The Wise Men
and
The Unknown God

MATHEW P. JOHN

Dear Susie
May the Lord guide
you to the ultimate
revelation of Christ

FOCUS INFINITY

Toronto   Los Angeles

The Wise Men and The Unknown God
A Spiritual Journey from the East to the West
Copyright © 2017 Mathew P John

ISBN-13: 978-0986705960

The author mostly relies on his personal knowledge on ancient
languages to translate the sacred scriptures of different religions.
Most verses of the Hindu/Buddhist scriptures are based on
translations available at www.sacred-text.com, Sikh scriptures at
www.srigurugranth.org, Islamic scriptures at www.Quran.com, (Sahih
International version), and Hebrew/Christian scriptures mostly from
NASB version of the Bible. The New American Standard
Bible® (NASB), Copyright © 1960, 1962, 1963, 1968, 1971, 1972,
1973, 1975, 1977, 1995 by The Lockman Foundation. Used by
permission. www.Lockman.org

Focus Infinity Press
Toronto. Los Angeles
www.focusinfinity.com

Editor   Keely Latcham Boeving
Cover Design Cizlini Arts
                based on an original painting by
                Joanne Mathew

"How can the world religions be so drastically different and yet also uncannily similar and possibly related? Isn't it incomprehensible that the great faiths are both strikingly contrasting but also remarkably overlapping and even convergent? Might these paradoxical observations be resolved because Jesus is both the unavoidable stumbling block that sets Christianity apart but yet perhaps also the one way that somehow they all point to? *The Wise Men and the Unknown God* invites readers on a journey to consider these questions in light of a gospel that challenges, even as it opens up conversation with, people in other faiths."

Dr. AMOS YONG,
Director, CMR, Fuller Theological Seminary
Author: *Hospitality and the Other:*
Pentecost, Christian Practices, and the Neighbor

"Author Eugene Petersen observed that we have two mental operations that work in tandem—explanation and imagination. And hardly anything grips our imagination as a well-written story, inviting us to enter the story and play our part in the unfolding drama. What an exciting way to learn about an otherwise ho hum topic—world religions. Read and enter."

Rev. Sunder Krishnan
Rexdale Alliance, Toronto
Author: *The Conquest of Inner Space*

"God is bigger than our boxes! Firmly planted in Jesus' claims of exclusivity for salvation, Mathew discovers "God's redemptive grace lurking in the dark and hidden corners of different religions." *The Wise Men and the Unknown God* will confirm and stretch your beliefs at the same time."

Dr. Craig Sider
President, New York City Leadership

"This book is a generous, thoughtful, nuanced, and compelling exploration of six faith traditions and their views of Jesus, written by a scholar who is himself a committed follower of Jesus. This is a book to share with your friends."

Dr. Richard Peace
Professor of Spiritual Formation, Fuller Theological Seminary
Author: *Noticing God*

"The book, birthed out of personal experience and passion, is an excellent resource for all of us to understand our neighbour's perspective and the gifts we all have to give one another. In a world where more compassion, respect and understanding is so desperately needed, *The Wise Men and the Unknown God* is a timely bridge in a sea of walls."

Christa Hesselink,
Author: *Life's Great Dare: Risking It All for the Abundant Life*

"*The Wise Men and the Unknown God* offers an incredible resource to people of all religious backgrounds, particularly Christians who are looking to understand world religions and how people can talk together in a respectful and thoughtful way about their beliefs. The author's breadth of knowledge, thoughtful insights and conversational approach are a very rare combination and make it easy for people to grasp the beliefs of world religions, learn from each other and also consider the life and message of Jesus in light of world religions. I highly recommend this book."

Tim Day
The City Movement,
Author: *God Enters Stage Left*

The author dared to proclaim Christ as the way, the truth and the life in a world culture that is not open to such claim... He describes how other religions picture Christ and anybody — not just Israel — could have access to father God, through Jesus Christ and be His friends and children with all the promises and its benefits that comes with faith in Christ, which is the only true way of Salvation.

Rev. Thomas Kutty
National Leader (Emeritus), The Foursquare Church in India.

"This book will lead you to your own personal encounters with Jesus, but in the process, will also help you discover the star that illuminates the path into an inclusive heavenly Jesus!"

Dr. Johnny Ramirez-Johnson
Professor of Anthropology, Fuller Theological Seminary

To

Joanne

best friend,
fiercest critic,
and
one true love.

CONTENTS

ACKNOWLEDGMENTS

The narrative of this book unfolds as a personal spiritual journey from the East to the West, which I embarked on years ago, both literally and figuratively. This journey took place in the company of many fellow pilgrims. You, my reader, are the last one I meet on this road; so let me start by thanking you for picking up this book.

The content of this book is drawn from a series of seminars on Christian response to world religions that I have been offering at various academic and ecclesiastical platforms currently available as "The Mosaic Course."

I want to thank the board of directors and the ministry partners of Focus Infinity Intercultural Outreach Network, the not-for-profit organization behind The Mosaic Course, for their unwavering support and constant encouragement, without which an endeavor of this magnitude would have been impossible to undertake. I also want to thank the co-writers of The Mosaic Course: John Bowen, Joshua Thambiraj, Thomas Leung, Mona Scrivens, Maria Short, Muhammad (Sam) Nasser, and Dan Stephenson, for enriching the course with insights from different cultural and theological perspectives.

The project was initially conceived of as a series of booklets written by different authors, but I decided to go back to the original content of my seminars and write it out as a "story." In this process I have drawn from many personal encounters I have had with people of different religious backgrounds. Although I have used creative license to alter their names and the details of these episodes, I want to gratefully acknowledge the significant contribution they have made to the content of this book.

I want to thank my close friends and confidants, Drew Logan and Jim Rhodes, for enriching my thought life, and covering it with prayer. My hikes with Jim on Mount Wilson, and prayer times with Drew at Sunset Boulevard were the weekly distractions I desperately needed during this long and arduous process of writing.

Coming straight out of a doctoral dissertation and an academic book project with a major publisher, I needed to reinvent my language, tone, and style for this book. My editor, Keely Boeving, helped me do just that, and much more. I want to thank her for being "invasive" and "pushy," by challenging me to frame my arguments from the perspective of the prospective reader, and prodding me to find the right balance between academic and "popular" writing.

The true inspiration for this book came from a fortuitous invitation I received from my favorite author, Philip Yancey, and his gracious wife Janet, to join them on a weeklong trip to India. I have since had the privilege to learn from the "Yancey I never knew"—an experience that has challenged me to approach a contentious topic like apologetics with an attitude of humility and grace. I am deeply indebted to their kindness and generosity, and grateful for their unmitigated support to my ministry.

I have dedicated this book to my wife, Joanne, who was providentially matched with me through a cosmic algorithm commonly called "arranged marriage." I want to thank her, not only for being my faithful partner for the last eighteen years and counting (it merits a big round of applause in itself, if you know me at all), but also for her creative contributions reflected in every page of this book. I also thank our gracious children, Hannah and Emma, for tolerating a writer-dad, who keeps swinging back and forth from alternate realities, even during family meals. I promise to do better, and vow to dedicate my next book to you.

Mathew P John

"Here I am, I have come—it is written about me in the scroll."

Psalms 40:7

PROLOGUE

My story begins on a cold December morning in a tiny village in southern India.

The celestial sound of the *Gayatri mantra* floats along the tender mist, waking up the world to a bright and blessed morning.

> *Om tat savitur varenyam*
> *Bhargo devasya dhîmahi*
> *Dhiyo yo nah prachodayât*

The age-old prayer of the sages fills the air with the profound presence of the sacred.

> Oh God! Creator of the universe,
> May we receive thy supreme light,
> May Thou guide our intellect in the right direction.

The Gayatri mantra is known as the mother of all mantras in Hinduism. It is an integral part of temple rituals, and a customary incantation at any auspicious occasion. This primeval chant has been the "morning alarm" for every Indian for generations.

The quest for *Savithur*, the Supreme Light, initiates the spiritual journey of a Hindu. During the initiation rites (*upanayana*), the priests recite the Gayatri mantra directly into the ears of their pupils. Once the initiates themselves perfect the chant, they are considered twice born (*dwijan*). They have stepped into a new realm of consciousness, and their spiritual journey is guided by the quest for the Supreme Light from now on.

As the soothing chants of the Gayatri mantra melt into my soul, a piercing voice explodes from a loud speaker:

> In Him was life; and the life was the light of men.
> And the light shineth in darkness;
> and the darkness comprehended it not . . .

The reading comes from a church building across the street from the Hindu temple. The curate is reciting from the Bible, in preparation for the commencement of the morning mass.

> . . . That was the true Light, which lighteth
> every man that cometh into the world.

I feel like I am in the middle of a conversation—a dialogue between two great world religions. The Scripture verses descending from the church-dome seem to answer the Vedic prayer rising from the temple-steeple. One searching for the Supreme Light that enlightens the universe; the other declaring its arrival into our dark and desolate world.

"I am the light of the world," says Jesus Christ.

Is the Christian Scripture responding to the prayers of the ancient sages? Lying there, as a boy of twelve, I begin to wonder.

FOLLOWING THE STAR

"I permitted Myself to be sought by those who did not ask for Me;
I permitted Myself to be found by those who did not seek Me.
I said, 'Here am I, here am I,' to a nation
which did not call on My name."

Isaiah 65:1

"Your eyes will see this and you will say,
'The Lord be magnified beyond the border of Israel!'"

Malachi 1:5

In the southern tip of India, there is a tiny state called Kerala. Sandwiched between an ocean and a mountain, it features one of the most scenic landscapes in the tropical region. The exquisite terrain of Kerala once inspired *National Geographic* to run an exclusive feature that described this land as "The Jewel of India's Malabar coast."[1]

I grew up in a small town in Kerala called Piravom. The word Piravom comes from the root word *piravi*, which literally means "birth" or "nativity." According to legends, Piravom is the hometown of one of the magi, or Wise Men, who visited Jesus at his birth.

India is the land of astrologers. At the time of Jesus' birth, it was one of the few cultures that had mastered the art of interpreting the cosmic connection between the stars and human destiny. It is believed that the Persian magi initially studied under Hindu sages, whom they described as the "magi of India."[2] The sudden appearance of a brilliant star, as recorded in the gospels, might have suggested to them the birth of an important person, inspiring them to take on an adventurous journey in search of the person.

The validity of this claim is still open for debate. But suffice it to say, the *Encyclopedia Britannica* postulates that at least one of the magi who visited Christ was from India, and this theory is widely accepted in the Christian tradition.[3] Today, Piravom maintains a thriving Christian community that traces its history all the way back to the time of the magi. It also has a majestic cathedral dedicated to the magi, aptly named "The Church of the Holy Kings."[4]

All things considered, one fact remains indisputable: the Wise Men of the East, the earliest religious figures to worship Jesus, did not belong to the so-called "Judeo-Christian" tradition. They were outsiders. They came from far outside the realm of the covenant God had established with Israel, His chosen nation.

How was this possible? How did the knowledge of the most pivotal moment in human history, God's descent into the human world, reach the Eastern world before it did the Promised Land? How did these Gentile diviners recognize the birth of the Messiah before the Jewish scribes and priests did?

We won't be able to answer these questions unless we are willing to reexamine some of the theological precepts we often take for granted. Let us start with a sacred tenet those of us of Judeo-Christian heritage hold very close to our heat: the election of Israel as God's chosen nation.

***

Is God a racist? I grew up thinking He was.

I was taught in Sunday school that the Jews are the "chosen people" of God. "Out of all the peoples on the face of the earth, the Lord has chosen you to be His treasured possession," says God to the Jews.[5] This didn't make sense to me. What kind of a God would choose one nation over others, and call them "My People"? What kind of a father would pick a favorite among his children?

As an Indian, God's preoccupation with the Jewish nation made me feel invisible and insignificant. How, I wondered, could God be so blatantly biased towards one particular ethnic group? If Jews are God's people, then who are Indians (or Asians, Africans, or Caucasians for that matter) to God? Why didn't He choose any of us?

Don't get me wrong. Growing up in India, known for one of the earliest settlements of the Jewish diaspora, I have had the privilege to have many Jewish friends.[6] They are a wonderful people, of course. But as a Sunday school kid, I did not understand why their story filled every page of the Bible, as if nothing happened elsewhere in the world. Why were they considered "special" in the eyes of God?

It was in the midst of this internal wrestling, when I was about fourteen, that an eye-opening event happened at my school.

I studied at a rural school in India, which enrolled over a thousand students from middle-class families. Funded by the local government, our student body did not have the luxury of organizing any type of recreational events. So we often turned to roadshow runners and street performers to provide us with our periodic dose of entertainment.

One day a traveling magician presented an impromptu show at our morning assembly. He started with token tricks, such as pulling out candies and balloons from an empty hat, and soon proceeded to a more formal routine.

In the middle of an act, the magician called for a volunteer from the audience. All of us looked at each other. No one dared to go. We had seen magicians tossing their assistants across the stage, cutting them in half, and even making them disappear. What if he tried one of those menacing tricks on us?

The magician called out again, this time warning that if no one volunteered, he was going to randomly pick an assistant out from the audience.

We crouched lower behind the seats as his eyes scanned the audience, avoiding eye contact as much as we could. After a few seconds of nerve-racking silence, we heard his voice:

"You, the one in the blue shirt, come up."

I looked up with a sigh of relief. Thank God, I was wearing a white shirt.

I turned around, looking in the direction the magician was motioning. There he was, the boy in the blue shirt—the chosen one. He was a dorky kid whom all the bullies loved to pick on. He usually sat in the back of the class, ate his lunch alone, and spent most of his recess hours in the bathroom. The audience began snickering the moment they saw who it was.

As the boy climbed on to the stage, the magician began pouring some milk into a glass, filling it up to the brim. He set it on a table in the center of the stage and turned towards his new assistant.

"You are going to drink this milk through the air," said the magician.

He handed an empty straw to the boy, who held it between his quivering lips.

"Drink up, my friend," commanded the magician, waving his wand over the glass of milk with an enchanting gesture.

The boy stood there, befuddled, for a long second. The glass was at least twenty-five feet away from him and he had only a six-inch straw. His predicament was becoming highly entertaining to all of us.

All he could do was suck in air through the straw, and that is what he did. Suddenly the magic began to unfurl. To our surprise, the milk in the glass started disappearing as he sucked on the straw. The audience gasped in disbelief. Was he actually siphoning the milk through thin air?

The milk finally reached the bottom of the glass. Even though he hardly knew what had just happened, the chosen one stood there triumphantly with a victorious smile on his face.

This would have been the end of the story. But the real magic happened only after the magician left the school premises.

That dorky, friendless kid in the blue shirt suddenly became a superstar in the school. How in the world could he have drunk that glass of milk unless he had acquired some mysterious power from the magician? We wondered.

The school journal ran a cover story on his extraordinary adventure. Girls began chasing their new heartthrob in the hallways. An entourage now protected the celebrity from his unruly fans. Even the teachers began to regale each other with the legend of the boy in the blue shirt.

A hero was born.

As far as the magician was concerned, the boy in the blue shirt was an arbitrary choice. He was not chosen because he was special. But he became special because he was chosen.

***

The history of Israel begins like most movie trailers: "One man, on a journey, to a land unknown . . ."

God picks a man. His name is Abraham. God establishes a covenant with him: "I will make you a great nation. I will make your name great, so you shall be a blessing."[7] Today, Abraham is considered a father figure to three major religions in the world—Judaism, Christianity, and Islam— the members of which surpass half the world's population.

The Jews claim that the covenant God gave to Abraham is applicable only to them because they alone are his descendants, his flesh and blood. In the same vein, Christians describe the Jews as the "chosen people of God." Theologians call this "the scandal of particularity."

This scandal hit home for me later in life, in a college Bible study group. I had an unexpected encounter with a young Palestinian Christian in one of the sessions. His sister had been brutally raped by an Israeli soldier in Gaza, and his older brother and mother were killed in subsequent raids conducted by the Israeli army.

"I will never accept them as the chosen people, no matter what the Bible says. I won't care if God Himself comes down and says that [expletive] to me," he sobbed, trying to bury his face inside his Bible.

The rest of us in the group knew he was wrong. We could have chided him with quotes from the Bible and a host of other books. Yet all of us, including a couple of Jewish Christians who were part of the group, sat quietly, numbed by his pain.

I come across similar predicaments in most conversations connected to the nation of Israel. The very mention of the word "Israel" spontaneously elicits two equal and opposite reactions: one group hates them for no apparent reason except that they exist, and another group adores them simply because they are the chosen people of God.

It is both a blessing and a curse to be the "chosen one."

***

Why did God choose Abraham over anyone else? I have no idea. Why did the magician choose the boy in the blue shirt? I don't know that either. One thing I do know, however, is that the act of choosing had nothing much to do with the merits of the chosen one.

The Hebrew Scriptures do not always paint a particularly flattering picture of Abraham. There is an incident, for example, where Abraham and his nomadic tribe arrive in the land of Egypt. He fears that his beautiful wife, Sarah, will attract unnecessary attention from the lustful eyes of the Pharaoh. If the king comes to know that she is married to him, his life will be in danger. So Abraham forces Sarah to pretend that she is his sister (which was partially true).

Later, as the story unfolds, Pharaoh finds out that he is about to commit adultery by marrying her. The conscience-stricken king cries out in distress: "What is this you have done to me? Why did you not tell me that she was your wife . . . so that I would take her for my wife?"[8]

Who is morally superior in this story—the chosen one who tried to trade his wife or the pagan king who refused to take the bait?

It is the mystery of God's election. He does not pick anyone based on his or her qualifications. God's choosing is always an act of grace.

God did not pick Abraham because he was special. But, like the boy in the blue shirt, Abraham became special because he was chosen.

Crucially, the arbitrary selection of one assistant does not imply the rejection of the rest of the audience. As a matter of fact, the non-chosen ones are the true beneficiaries of the act being performed by the chosen one.

Our rational mind is trained to think in a dualistic paradigm. We tend to look at the selection of something in conjunction with a "rejection" of everything else. But that is not necessarily true in this case. Both the volunteer and the audience are equally important to the Magician.

In the story told by the Hebrew Scriptures, Abraham is the boy in the blue shirt. He was called to demonstrate God's magical power to the rest of the world. God's covenant with him, if you read it closely, came with a footnote: "In you *all the families of the earth* shall be blessed" (emphasis mine). In other words, the Jews were chosen for the sake of the Gentiles, and were meant to be a channel of God's blessings to the rest of the world.

Of course, the status of the chosen one has to be special. Whatever happens to the assistant invariably affects the course of the magic act. So the Magician has to make sure that the assistant is rendered whole and invincible throughout the act. To do so, he establishes a "covenant" with him—a binding promise between the Magician and the chosen one that ensures the best possible performance of the magic act.

The Jews are born into the center stage of God's magic show, as it unfolds in time and space. A Jew is, by default, God's lovely assistant, and is equipped to function as a channel of His grace to "all the families of the earth."

Here is the catch. If we think that being "chosen" is a privileged status that comes with a platinum credit card and special lounge access, we couldn't be farther from the truth. "You only have I chosen among all the families of the earth," says Amos, the prophet. But the verse that follows this promise is rather ominous: "Therefore, I will punish you for all your iniquities."[9]

In our morally compromised world, chosen ones tend to have privileged status, and they get away with all the mistakes they make. But the Jews are not called into a privilege; rather, they are assigned a responsibility. The responsibility comes with a certain set of privileges, of course, but only because they are necessary to accomplish the given mission.

The Magician has to pay a heavy price even for the most inadvertent mistakes made on the stage. Therefore the assistant has to be flawless and exemplary. That is the burden of his calling. The audience, on the other hand, need not be perfect, and their imperfections remain unobserved.

The chosen one has to be perfected on a continual basis. This is perhaps why the Jews have become the most persecuted people in the world, and Israel the most scandalous nation in human history.

Now I say under my breath: "Thank You, God, for NOT choosing Indians."

Let the boy in the blue shirt take the limelight. I would rather watch him from the comfort of my balcony seat. I don't complain because I know God is equally interested in me, and His magic act is being performed for my sake as much as it is for the sake of everyone else in the world.

***

It is an irony that the "exclusive" covenant God established with Israel was, in fact, "inclusive" at its very heart. Although it was addressed to Abraham, as we have already seen, the covenant was meant for "all families of the earth." In other words, the selection of Israel does not imply God's exclusivity to a particular nation; it rather demonstrates a sweeping inclusivity of the whole wide world.

God's first covenant came to Noah, elegantly wrapped in a rainbow. This was an "everlasting covenant between God and *every living creature of all flesh that is on the earth*" (emphasis mine).[10] But the universal language of the covenant changed its tone and vocabulary by the time it reached Abraham. The Abrahamic covenant was addressed to a specific group of people at a specific time in history. Why, just a few short generations after the covenant with Noah, was God suddenly disinterested in the rest of the world? Why did He decide to work exclusively with a particular racial group?

We find the answer to this question in the book of Genesis. In an episode titled "Babel," we see a cultural calamity of seismic proportion happening in the world. Not so long after Noah's descendants repopulate the earth following the great flood, the people decide to build a tower to protect themselves from future disasters. It triggers a de-globalization process of sorts, resulting in cultural chaos and emergence of unique languages.

God could not have communicated to this cacophonous culture by picking up a megaphone and yelling at the crowd. He had to choose a specific group and entrust them with His message, hoping they would communicate it to the rest of the world. For reasons best known to Him, this is the way God prefers to operate in the world even today.

In any case, God chose Abraham, the boy in the blue shirt, as the bearer of His message. And He sent him out as His ambassador to the world. The tone of the revelation now changed from "universal" to "particular," but the intended recipient of the covenant remained the same—"all families of the earth."

Abraham's descendants soon deceived themselves, however, into thinking that they were God's personal favorites. They overlooked the fact that "being chosen" had brought them not into a privileged status but into a crucial responsibility. The assistant ignored the audience and began to indulge in his newfound stardom.

The prophets kept reminding Israel that their mission was to be "a light for the Gentiles" so that they could bring God's salvation "to the ends of the earth."[11] There are other "people of God" in the world, they declared, apart from the Jewish nation. In the prophetic visions God addressed the Egyptians, the archenemy of the Israelites, "My people."[12]

The God who delivered Israel from the oppression of Egypt also delivered "Egypt from its oppressors." The God who promised the Messiah for Israel also promised "a savior and a champion" for Egypt. He who brought Israel out of Egypt also brought "Arameans from Kir" and "Philistines from Caphtor."[13]

The sacred temple in Jerusalem, the epicenter of God's presence on earth, was not a Jewish temple, the prophets declared; it was rather a "house of prayer for all nations."[14]

The Israelites, however, didn't particularly want to hear about the inclusive nature of God's message. Egyptians, Arameans, and Philistines were all hard-nosed enemies of Israel, sworn to wipe out the chosen people from planet earth. Egyptians enslaved Israel for nearly four centuries; Arameans fought the kings of Israel sporadically. Remember the iconic evil giant, Goliath? He was a Philistine. How could the God of Israel act as an agent of salvation in the history of these savage nations?

As one theologian puts it, Israel "largely forgot the fact that they were meant to be a missionary nation and their calling was meant to be translated into dynamic outreach."[15] So God scattered them among the nations. The Jews became a nomadic people wandering all over the world, moving from one tent to the next. God remained faithful, however, dispensing His grace and glory through them wherever they went.

When the assistant walked off the stage and wandered among the audience, the Magician walked with him. As a result, everyone got to see the magic, up close and personal. In a strange and mysterious way, the Magician used even the apparent flaw in his assistant's character as an opportunity to demonstrate his dedication and commitment to the audience. The flickering flames of the "light of salvation" suddenly illumined the whole auditorium.

The Bible is the story of God's magic act in the world, but it is written from the perspective of Israel. It is a view of the stage given to us through the eyes of His assistant. It is the best narrative we can have and the only one we need. But it does not mean that we have the whole picture. There are numerous eyes staring at the stage, and they all have their own stories of the magic to tell. But in the end, the magic transcends all narratives; God goes beyond all stories.

***

What if God were to ask a televangelist to go and preach repentance to the jihadists wreaking havoc in the Middle East? God once asked something very similar to a prophet named Jonah. In fact, the poor preacher was forced against his will to go and preach to the Assyrian city of Nineveh.

"Should I not have compassion for Nineveh?" God asks Jonah.[16] Jonah does not respond. The answer in his mind would have been a resounding "NO."

First of all, the Assyrians didn't worship the God of Israel. So why, Jonah might have wondered, should He be interested in their miserable lives? Secondly, they were a notoriously wicked nation that, by the standards of earthly justice, deserved neither mercy nor compassion. Thirdly, they were the same people who would march into the Promised Land just a few decades later and obliterate the kingdom of Israel from the face of the earth.[17] Why would God want to save them?

And yet Jonah does, eventually, do what the Lord asked him to do. He goes to Ninevah and delivers the message, ultimately leading the Assyrians to repent from their evil ways. This is only one of the many instances in the Hebrew scriptures where God intervenes on behalf of people who are outside the chosen nation of Israel.

In the Chronicles of the kings of Israel, we meet the Egyptian king Neco leading a campaign against the Chaldeans. Josiah, the king of Judah, comes against him at Megiddo. But Neco does not want to wage war against Judah. "What have we to do with each other, O King of Judah?" asks Neco. "I am not coming against you today but against the house with which I am at war, and God has ordered me to hurry. Stop for your own sake from interfering with God who is with me, so that He will not destroy you."[18]

It is important to remember that Josiah was one of the very few righteous kings of Judah. Unlike most of his ancestors, he zealously followed the law of God. While Josiah reigned, God's favor was upon Judah and its king. So what authority does Neco possess to be God's spokesperson to Josiah? If God wants to speak to the king of Judah, He should rather send a legitimate prophet from His fold, not an alien king who worships the idols of Isis and Osiris.

Naturally, Josiah discredits the counsel of Neco, and marches against Egypt. This decision happens to cost him not only his kingdom but also his life. In the surprising climax of the story we realize that the Egyptian king was, in fact, speaking on behalf of the God of Israel. This is how the narrator describes the event: "nor did he listen to the words of Neco from the mouth of God."[19] The words that came out of the mouth of the pagan king, we are told, actually were the very words of God.

In another instance, Abraham comes across a pagan priest named Melchizedek.[20] He greets Abraham in the name of his god, *El Elyon*.[21] Abraham does not insist that he should be greeted in the name of the "real" God, Yahweh. Instead, he gives his tithe, God's portion of his wealth, to Melchizedek. Later in the Scriptures, David prophesies that the Jewish Messiah would come as a priest in the line of Melchizedek, not in the line of traditional Levitical priesthood.[22] Is the God of Abraham the same as the god of Melchizedek? Could it be that Yahweh and El Elyon are two different names of the same God? We will consider many such questions over the course of our journey.

In the pages of the Bible we meet many Gentile characters who seem to play active roles in God's redemptive plan for the world. Jethro, Moses' father-in-law, was once a priest to the pagan deities of Midian. But he acted as chief counsel to Moses in the Exodus mission.[23] Rahab, a prostitute, and Ruth, a Moabite, were women born miles outside the sphere of God's covenant. Yet they became pivotal figures in the history of Israel, finding their way into the genealogy of the ultimate Jewish hero, King David (and of Jesus Christ). The Queen of Sheba was commended by Jesus himself for her eagerness to learn from the wisdom of Solomon. King Hiram of Tyre, a pagan king, partnered with Solomon in building the first Temple of Jerusalem.[24] King Cyrus of Persia, another Gentile ruler, received a divine appointment to build the second Jewish Temple. Prophets called him "anointed" and addressed him, "God's signet ring."[25]

It seems to me that God has been actively involved in the history of many nations outside the geographical borders of Israel. His reach includes the whole world. He is certainly interested in all of us.

Salvation may have been "from" the Jews, but it is not exclusively "for" the Jews.

***

In the gospels of Mark and Luke, we find an encounter between Jesus' disciples and a young man who performs miracles in his name.[26] Impressed by his devotion and dedication, the disciples offer him an invitation to join their team.

Being part of the disciples' band meant working closely with Jesus. It would have been a dream come true for an aspiring minister. But the man declines their invitation. A Christ-follower who refuses an invitation to "literally" follow Christ? How could someone refuse to follow Jesus and still perform miracles in his name?

The disciples report the incident to Jesus: "We tried to prevent him because he was not following us." After all, someone needs to safeguard the community against unaccredited preachers and their heretical teachings.

Jesus' response, however, is sobering:

"Do not hinder him," says Jesus. "For he who is not against us is for us."

In another instance, Jesus said that he had many sheep "which are not of this fold."[27] Is this young man one of those sheep from the "other" fold? What, I find myself wondering, is this mysterious other fold? Is there a group of sheep that has never met the shepherd, yet belongs to him anyway? Can these sheep recognize the shepherd's voice even if they have never seen him in person?

I can offer various conjectures, but in the end, no one has any convincing answers to these questions. I have learned one thing from this story, however. God's grace cannot be confined to the boundaries of a visible community. As passionate as I am about my Church and the purity of its doctrines, who am I to say that whoever does not follow Christ with me, does not follow him at all?

This kind of exclusive thinking is not limited to the Israelites or the disciples of Jesus. Today many Christians have fallen into the same trap that tripped the children of Abraham. We are the recipients of the New Covenant. We are now the chosen ones.[28] We also delude ourselves, at times, into thinking that those who are outside the realm of this covenant do not matter to God at all.

It is true that God's offer of salvation is in one sense "exclusive"—it is not revealed to all religions and cultures. But it is also "inclusive" in the sense that it originates in one community and flows into others. Few are chosen, so that many may receive.

The universal reach of the New Covenant was first revealed to the church when God asked Peter to visit a man named Cornelius.[29] This man was not a Christian, yet he was a "devout man" who "feared God with all his household" and "prayed to God" continually. It comes as a big surprise to Peter to know that God is interested in the prayers of those who are neither Jews nor Christians. He gets a rude awakening through a dramatic vision, in which God commands, "what God has cleansed, no longer consider unholy." This incident was likely foremost on Peter's mind as he wrote in his epistle that God does not wish "for any to perish, but for all to come to repentance."[30]

To be elected in Jesus Christ means to be incorporated into God's mission of establishing His Kingdom on earth.

The Kingdom of God is meant for all people. "There is no difference between Jew and Greek," says Paul. "For whosoever shall call upon the name of the Lord shall be saved."[31] This "inclusive exclusivity" of the gospel is further amplified in his letters, which reiterate the fact that God is "the Savior of all men, especially of believers."[32] He desires that "all people everywhere should repent,"[33] and for "all men to be saved and to come to the knowledge of the truth."[34]

As a Christian, I believe that God's supreme revelation comes to humanity in the person of Jesus Christ. I am now entrusted with the task of taking it to the four corners of the world. Like Israel became "the light to the Gentiles,"[35] Christians are appointed "the light of the world."[36] The most important thing to remember is that salvation is a call to responsibility, not to privilege. We are not chosen for our own sakes, but for the sakes of others.

***

"In Him we live and move and have our being."[37]

One of the most beautiful verses in the Bible, I often hear it quoted in liturgies, benedictions, and worship songs. I see it printed on bumper stickers and painted on church buildings. In a silent yet eloquent voice, this verse reminds us of the invisible presence of God in our everyday life.

Not many people know that this verse actually comes from a pagan source. It is an excerpt from *Cretica*, a poem written by the Greek philosopher Epimenides, in the seventh century BCE.[38] Here is the full version:

> They fashioned a tomb for you, holy and high one,
> Cretans, always liars, evil beasts, idle bellies.

But you are not dead: you live and abide forever,
For in you we live and move and have our being.[39]

The "Holy and High God" of this poem in whom "we live and move and have our being" is not the Jewish or Christian God. He is, in fact, the Greek god Zeus.

I wonder why Paul decided to incorporate the voice of a pagan poet into his Holy Spirit inspired sermon. Further, why would Luke, the writer of the Acts, record it in a book that we revere as the "Word of God"? How could a pagan prophecy find its way into the sacred Scriptures of Christianity?

The episode starts with Paul exploring the city of Athens as he waits for his colleagues to join him.[40] The idols in the city provoke his spirit. However, instead of condemning their idolatry, Paul goes on to affirm Athenians' zeal for God. He then transitions into a "show and tell" using one of their own idols for an object lesson.

The god at the center of Paul's message is "*Agnostos Theos*," or "the unknown god." The legend behind the unknown god was not unknown to the Greeks.[41] It had its origins in a plague that spread through Greece at the time of Epimenides, which created a nationwide pandemonium. People offered sacrifices to appease the angry gods as usual, but the plague continued to spread. There must be yet another god who was still not pleased, they thought, but no one knew who he was. So they built new altars in the name of an "unknown" god and offered blood sacrifices. As the story goes, the epidemic came to an immediate stop, and a new god found his way into the crowded Greek pantheon.

"What you worship in ignorance, this I proclaim to you," says Paul to the Athenians, pointing to the altar of the unknown god.[42] He is not preaching a new god; instead he is revealing the "hidden" God embedded in their own religion. The unknown god of the Athenians, all of a sudden, becomes a signpost that points to the God of the Bible.

This, of course, is not Paul's endorsement of idol worship, nor does it show his indulgence in syncretic missional practices. It is rather an affirmation of God's ubiquitous presence in every religion and in every culture.

If the God of Israel revealed Himself outside the geographical borders of His covenant, it only makes sense that the "good news" of the arrival of His Son would spill outside the traditional boundaries of the Church and stream into the hearkening ears of genuine seekers everywhere, including my ancestors—the Wise Men of the East.

What if I could hear what they heard? What if I could see what they saw? What if I could follow the star that guided their path?

My quest for the Supreme Light led me to a personal pilgrimage in the footsteps of the Wise Men. It was an exhilarating expedition through six major religions in the world, looking for the glimpses of redemptive revelations God has embedded in their sacred narratives.

As my journey progressed, the unknown god lurking behind the dark and hidden corners of world religions began to unveil himself. In the path lit by the shining rays of the Supreme Light, I chanced upon many fellow pilgrims who followed Jesus without actually following his followers. I communed with many who are in communion with Christ without ever being in the community of his disciples.

I discovered, to my surprise, that the followers of other religions possess a respectful, if not reverential, understanding of the One whom the Wise Men were after. The Jews consider him a rabbi who claimed to be their Messiah; the Muslims, a prophet; the Sikhs, a guru or a *sant*; the Buddhists, a bodhisattva; the Hindus, an avatar.

I am not one of the Wise Men, of course, but I am here to accompany you on a trail set by them. All I can promise you on this journey is some stories for the road. They will help you discover the vignettes of truth God has woven into the spiritual fabric of all cultures and all religions. Who knows, you might even run into the unknown god along the way!

2

THE DESCENT OF GOD

"For the preservation of good, for the destruction of evil,
for the establishment of righteousness,
I come into being in age after age."

Bhagavad Gita 4:7

If you walk into the Kwik-E-Mart store in a town called Springfield, you will meet the most well known Hindu in all of America. His name is Apu Nahasapeemapetilon—originally a PhD in computer science from India, he currently operates a convenience store in the town. He lives in a house adjacent to the store with his wife, Manjula, and their eight children.

Unfortunately you won't be able to meet this delightful family in person, unless you are a cartoon character. The Nahasapeemapetilons are characters on *The Simpsons*, the most popular animated series in television history.

There are more than one billion Hindus in the world today, many of them familiar to the Western world—from

Mahatma Gandhi to Mindy Kaling.[1] As I write this book, Microsoft and Google, the two major software empires in the world, are headed by CEOs who are Hindus.[2] Yet it is often Apu from the animated world who shapes the popular perception of Hinduism in the West.

According to the Pew Research Center, Hinduism is the third largest religion in the world. But that is merely statistics. In my opinion, the influence of Hinduism in our culture goes far beyond facts and figures. Let me explain.

Ask random people you meet on the street if they have heard the terms *"yoga," "karma,"* or *"avatar."* I bet the answer in most cases is going to be "yes." Now ask them if they know what *"lectio divina,"* "sanctification," or "incarnation" mean. Most likely they will roll their eyes. Here is the clue: the first three words come from the theological vernacular of Hinduism; the last three are the equivalent terms in Christian vocabulary.

In a *Newsweek* article appropriately titled *"We Are All Hindus Now,"* Lisa Miller writes: "America is not a Christian nation. . . . Recent poll data shows that conceptually, at least, we are slowly becoming more like Hindus and less like traditional Christians in the ways we think about God, ourselves, each other, and eternity." Miller bases her argument on the observations made by Stephen Prothero, professor of religion at Boston University, who also notes that "the American propensity for 'the divine-deli-cafeteria religion' is "very much in the spirit of Hinduism."[3]

The essence of Hinduism is encapsulated in the phrase *"Sanatana Dharma,"* which literally means "Universal Law" or "Universal Duty." In the Hindu worldview, all religions are of the same essence and are different paths to the same destination. A Hindu, therefore, has the freedom to draw elements from any religion, with no need for commitment to a specific doctrine. In other words, Hinduism is not a creedal religion. One is free to pick and choose what he or she wants to believe in this "divine-deli-cafeteria."

"If God is everywhere and can be worshipped anywhere, why do you want to build a temple in North America?" I asked a Hindu friend of mine who was championing a multimillion-dollar temple construction project in North America. "If all paths lead to the same destination, can't you worship in a church or in a mosque?"

"It is true that we Hindus believe all religions are equal," my friend responded with a playful smile.

"But Hinduism is more equal than the others."

I joined the laugh.

Although it does not believe in proselytization, Hinduism aggressively promotes its worldview, often under the guise of what we now call "New Age spirituality." Today there are many organizations—"Self-Realization Fellowship," "International Society for Krishna Consciousness," to name a few—that are engaged in enthusiastically advocating the Hindu cause in the Western world.

***

"I am a Hindu."

Julia Roberts, Hollywood actress and American sweetheart, declared to the press in 2010. It seemed part of a publicity campaign for one of her movies at the time, but it turns out that Roberts diligently practices her newfound faith even today.[4]

27

How can a white woman born in the Bible Belt and raised Catholic suddenly become a Hindu? We are prone to wonder. The fact is that Roberts is not the only celebrity spokesperson for Hinduism in the West. We know that the members of *The Beatles* often retreated to an ashram in India, submitted to Vedic teachings, and practiced transcendental meditation techniques. They even appointed a Hindu monk, Mahirshi Mahesh Yogi, as their spiritual director. It is also no secret that the founder of Apple, Steve Jobs, ascribed the rediscovery of his life's meaning and purpose to an enlightening spiritual encounter he had in India.

Our conception of what it means to be a Hindu has changed over time. The word *Hindu* literally means a native of India. It originates from the Persian word *Hind*, and is a name the Iranian invaders ascribed to the people of the Indus Valley River and beyond. Therefore, the term Hindu indicates a race or ethnicity more than a religion.

In that sense, Julia Roberts can never be a Hindu; but I, as a native-born Indian, am one without even realizing it.

Of course, we use the term "Hindu" in a different sense today, to describe the adherents of a religion that we call "Hinduism." Once again, the irony remains. Hinduism, in reality, is an amalgamation of various religious beliefs and practices discovered as part of the Indus valley civilization, which date all the way back to 3000 BCE.

Hinduism is the only major world religion with no known founder. It is more appropriate to say that the Persians "invented" the Hindu religion. They used Hinduism as a religious term to distinguish their monotheistic Islamic faith from a myriad of polytheistic religions practiced by the indigenous people of the country. For this reason and others, there is no sharp distinction between religion and culture in Hinduism.

It is quite easy to see how Hinduism became seductive to the postmodern West. It is an all-embracing religion, encompassing a wide spectrum of belief systems. It is so universalistic in its ideology that it validates not only the traditional monotheistic and polytheistic beliefs but also a belief in the non-existence of (a personal) God. All streams of knowledge, including atheism, are genuine paths that will eventually lead us to the Supreme Light.

It can be argued that anyone who believes in virtually anything can be a Hindu. "Whatever celestial form a devotee seeks to worship with faith, I steady the faith of such a devotee in that form," says the Bhagavad Gita, the Holy scripture of Hinduism. "Endowed with faith, the devotee worships a particular celestial god and obtains the objects of desire. But in reality I alone arrange these benefits."[5] Judged by this standard, a Christian who is passionately devoted to Christ can be just as good a Hindu as a Muslim who reverentially bows down before Allah.

Yes, Julia Roberts is a Hindu. But in the true context of Hinduism, so is the Pope.

***

The film adaptation of the Booker Prize-winning novel *Life of Pi* received eleven Oscar nominations in 2013. It is the coming-of-age story of a Hindu boy named Pi, who searches for God in all places, including temples, mosques, and churches. He eventually comes up with a hybrid god that is more like the *pi* of mathematics—an unresolved number or an indefinable symbol. Mathematicians have never fully understood pi, yet it does not stop them from churning out equations or formulae with pi. It works for them; that is what matters. This is a great model to frame the pragmatic spirituality of Hindu religion.

The foundational doctrine of Hinduism is something we could describe as "monistic pantheism." It is best encapsulated in the phrase: "All is one; all is God."

To be honest, I have never really understood the meaning of this phrase. Monism argues that God is not "the other"; He/She/It is a Universal Spirit that exists within all of us. You and I are of the same divine essence. I am God; so are you. Pantheism, on the other hand, believes in multiple gods who are characteristically different from each other.

Hinduism is known to the world as a pantheistic religion in the sense that it possesses an elaborate pantheon of gods, up to 330 million. However, all these gods are various manifestations of one Supreme Consciousness, called the *Brahman*. According to the Vedas, the ancient scriptures of Hinduism:

> *Ekam Sat Vipra, Bahuda Vadanti.* [6]
> (That which exists is One:
> sages call it by various names.)

There is only one reality. God and human beings are essentially one and are all part of the same existence. Any apparent distinction between them is caused by a phenomenon called *maya*, or illusion.

The so-called material world we see around us is nothing but a semblance created by maya. The time-space continuum in which we live, and even the appearance of our own individuality, is all part of this illusion. There is neither you nor I; Brahman is all there is. We don't realize this truth because of *avidya* (ignorance), our inability to comprehend the nature of maya.

Avidya is the term in Hindu philosophy that comes closest to what we call "sin" in other religious traditions. Swami Vivekananda once said, "Sinner . . . it is a sin to call man so."[7] We are divine souls residing inside physical bodies. We behave inappropriately because we don't realize our divinity. It is not sin, but avidya is what we need to overcome in order to eradicate evil and suffering in the world.

According to Hinduism, we are trapped in the epicenter of a grand illusion called the "*samsara* cycle"—the cycle of birth, death, and rebirth. When a person dies, the soul leaves the body and is reincarnated into a new body. So our empirical personhood is nothing but an illusion. The moment we realize this truth, we will be "enlightened." When an enlightened person dies, he or she escapes the samsara cycle and enters *moksha*, a state in which the individual soul merges with the Universal Soul.

If everything is part of a cosmic whole, who am I really? One might wonder. If my identity is an illusion, how can I be responsible for my own actions? If everything is an illusion, isn't God himself one? Hinduism does not seem to worry about such existential or theological questions.

The only way I can conceive of moksha—the ultimate union with the Universal Soul—is in terms of a personal relationship between God and myself. But if the Universal Soul and the individual soul have no personal attributes, where is the room for a meaningful relationship between the two? This dilemma creates a proverbial "God-shaped hole" in my heart as I journey through Hinduism.

"If you believe in everything," says Pi's father, "you believe in nothing."

***

I lived in India for well over two decades, but I had never seen a yoga studio until I stepped into one in Chicago. I was there to pick up a friend who was a part time yoga guru and a part time real estate agent. He waxed eloquently on the commercial potential of yoga and explained to me how easy it was to make a lucrative income teaching it to the "white folks." I was surprised because, as far as I knew, he had no training in yoga, nor was he an expert in any form of physical or spiritual disciplines. While in college his athletic abilities were practically as nonexistent as my own.

"I cook up my own version. That is what everybody does," said the guru with a smirk on his face. "At least I am from India. It gives me credibility."

Perhaps to get rid of his guilt, he later helped me, anonymously, write a proposal for a television documentary on yoga. Our documentary was an exposé of the billion-dollar self-help industry in North America and a satirical look at the transformation of yoga from being a religious ritual in the East to a fitness regimen in the West.

Did I say religious ritual? Yes. That is exactly what true yoga is. The spiritual and the physical are so inextricably blended in yoga that one cannot exist without the other. The word yoga itself means "being yoked together." It is a process by which one yokes his or her individual soul with the Universal Soul. The one who achieves this eternal union becomes a *yogi*.

In its original form, yoga is called *Ashtanga yoga* or "yoga with eight limbs."[8] The yoga most people practice in a typical studio today incorporates *asanas* (postures) and *pranayamas* (breathing), which are only two of these eight limbs. Most versions skip the first two—*yama* and *niyama*, which deal with moral and spiritual disciplines that are essential to the proper integration of the rest of the limbs. For this reason, we titled our documentary "Yoga: The Lost Limbs."[9]

There are predominantly four types of yogas, which are also described as four *margas* (paths). What we have been discussing so far is *Raja* or "royal" yoga. It uses psycho-physical exercises for invoking the dormant psychic energy within us to unite our human and divine natures. There are many subdivisions within Raja yoga: *tantric* yoga, which uses magical chants and sexual imagery; *kundalini* yoga, which draws up the kundalini (serpent) power through the spinal column, and so on. Some of these techniques are considered black magic, as they originate from the "forbidden" Vedas of Hinduism.[10] The practice can be so dangerous that if the attempt is bungled, it can result in psychosis or other types of neurotic disorders.

In addition to Raja, another type of yoga is *Karma* yoga, or the road to union through action or work. It emphasizes performing one's tasks diligently, so that his or her *dharma* (duty) becomes a vehicle of transcendence.

The key concept behind this practice is that of *nishkama karma* (disinterested action), whereby duty is performed with no concern about its consequences. "He who does the task dictated by duty, caring nothing for the fruit of action, he is a yogi," says Lord Krishna.[11]

Whatever we do with a selfish motive adds an extra layer to our ego, thereby further removing us from the Universal

Soul. On the other hand, every selfless deed we perform removes a layer of ego, until there is no barrier that separates us from the divine.[12]

As you might have noticed already, neither Karma yoga nor Raja yoga mandates the recognition of a divine figure in religious practice. In order to understand the concept of God in Hinduism, therefore, we need to go to the next two: *Jnana* yoga (the way of knowledge) and *Bhakti* yoga (the way of devotion).

***

"Where is God? How can I see Him?" a son asks his father.

The father hands him a pinch of salt. He then asks him to go and mix it in a cup of water.

"Where is the salt now?" asks the father.

"I cannot see it. The salt and water have become one."

"As the salt is in the water, we are one with the Universal Spirit. Just as there is no difference between the salt and the water there is no difference between you and God. Thou art That!"

The above is a popular story from the Hindu Upanishads, commentaries to the Vedas.[13] The phrase "Thou art That" (*Tat tvam Asi*) defines the foundational principle of Jnana yoga, the path to union with the Universal Soul through knowledge.

Jnana yoga conceives God as a formless Self with no personal attributes, often called *Nirguna* Brahman. God is not a He or a She but a "That"—a transcendent reality that encompasses everything that exists in the universe. The essence of Brahman is *Satchitananda*: infinite being (*Sat*), infinite consciousness (*Chit*), and infinite bliss (*Ananda*).

If the Universal Soul is Brahman, an individual soul is called *atman*. The realization that the atman and the Brahman are the same ("*Aham Brahma Asmi,*" or "I am Brahman") [14] brings "enlightenment." Enlightenment leads to moksha at death, where the atman is liberated from the samsara cycle and eternally merged into Brahman.

Jnana yoga generally stands against all forms of worship and devotion. Salvation comes from within; we do not need the help of a deity to achieve moksha. In other words, we are our own saviors.

Even though there are no savior-figures in this stream of Hinduism, there are "guides" available to help us on our path to enlightenment and, eventually, to moksha. Such a spiritual guide is called a *guru*. A guru is more than a teacher or an expert; for an aspirant, he is a conduit to divinity. He not only imparts knowledge but also embodies it.

Most Hindus consider a guru as a personification of the divine itself. He is often addressed as *gurudeva* (guru the god). The students are taught to recite the popular mantra "*matha pitha guru daivatam,*" on the first day of their school, which literally means, "Mother, Father, and Teacher are to be revered as gods themselves." The relationship between a guru and his students is similar to that of a deity and the devotees.

Most Hindus consider Jesus an enlightened guru who taught individual souls how to walk the path to moksha. He is someone who can help us overcome the evil of ignorance (*avidya*) and find the true path to enlightenment.

Followers of both Jnana yoga and Karma yoga accept Jesus as a great moral teacher, and they often quote his Sermon on the Mount in their ethical discourses. Great social reformers of India such as Raja Ram Mohan Roy and Mahatma Gandhi were inspired by the idea of nonviolence in Jesus' teachings and they incorporated it in their fight against social evils such as burning of the widows (*sati*) and segregation of the untouchables (*dalits*).

A Hindu may also consider Jesus a yogi who displayed the perfect union between divinity and humanity. His path was the most absolute form of renunciation, like that of *sadhus*, the wandering holy men of India. Swami Vivekananda described Jesus as a *sannyasi*, an ascetic who withdraws from the pleasures of the material world in order to practice meditation and contemplation. The time Jesus spent in the wilderness is characteristic of the disciplines of a yogi. When Jesus said, "I and the Father are one" he was, according to Hindus, speaking of the highest form of mystical union between an individual soul and the Universal Soul that only a yogi can experience.

***

I have lectured on Hinduism in many academic platforms. The Hindu students who attend my lectures would ferociously take notes up to this point. Most of what I have shared, believe it or not, is news to them. Why? The religion practiced by an average Hindu is diametrically different from what we have learned so far.

While philosophical Hinduism remains a hot topic in intellectual discourses, most Hindus follow devotional Hinduism, which, like most other religions, involves worshipping personal deities and observing religious rituals. Armchair philosophers may have the luxury to sit and contemplate on the nature of cosmic illusion, but ordinary people live in the "real" world, and they need real solutions to real problems. Religion, therefore, needs personal gods.

This is where Bhakti yoga, the path to union through devotion, makes its grand entrance. At the very heart of devotional Hinduism is the belief in One God who has revealed Himself since the beginning of creation:

> The All-Maker is vast in mind and vast in strength.
> He is the one who forms, who sets in order and
> Who is the highest image.[15]

The God of Bhakti yoga is not an impersonal Absolute but a Supreme Person. He is not the Nirguna Brahman of Jnana yoga but the *Saguna* Brahman, God with personal attributes:

> With eyes on all sides and mouths on all sides,
> With arms on all sides and feet on all sides,
> The One God created the sky and the earth,
> Fanning them with his arms.[16]

Bhakti yoga believes in God's "otherness" from the rest of the creation. If one needs to be devoted to God, God cannot be oneself. In other words, the creator and the creation have to be distinct entities.

The God of Bhakti yoga is not the apathetic, immutable Universal Self of the Jnana yoga; He is a "person" interested in entering into a meaningful relationship with His creation. In Hindu mythology, this one God, often called *Iswara* or *Bhagavan*,[17] manifests himself in the form of three distinct personal gods: Brahma (notice the difference between Brahman), Vishnu, and Siva. Together they are called the *Trimurthy*. As the sacred scriptures suggest, "the Supreme Spirit hath three conditions. In the form of Brahma, he is the Creator, and in the form of Vishnu he is the Preserver, and in his form as Rudra (Siva), he is the Destroyer of the Universe!"[18] Iswara is constantly engaged in the action of creation, preservation, and destruction through the Trimurthy.[19]

Although the concept of Trimurthy sounds very similar to the Christian idea of a Triune God, in fact, these theologies are very different. In the Trinity, one divine nature expresses itself in three distinct persons. But in Trimurthy, the one being manifests itself as three individual gods who operate independently of each other.

The God of Bhakti yoga, however, interacts with His devotees in an intimately personal way, calling them into a loving relationship with Him:

> Always think of me, be devoted to me,
> Worship me, and offer obeisance to me.
> Doing so, you will certainly come to me.
> This is my pledge, for you are very dear to me.[20]

What prevents the devotees from entering into this relationship is not avidya; rather, it is their personal offenses, akin to what we call "sin" in other religions. The worshippers can plead on the love of God, relating to Him as a father, a friend, or even as a lover:

> As a father tolerates his son,
> A friend forgives his friend, and
> A lover pardons the beloved,
> Please forgive me of my offences.[21]

Bhakti yoga portrays God also as a gracious and compassionate savior. Salvation is not the result of human effort, but it is a gift of God. His grace is not earned by one's effort, but is freely given, thus defying the karmic laws.

Abandon all varieties of dharmas
And simply surrender unto me alone.
I shall liberate you from all sinful reactions;
Do not fear.[22]

Moksha, in Bhakti yoga, is not disappearing into an impersonal Spirit but losing oneself in the intimacy with God. "In Bhakti theology, liberation does not appear to be the outcome of yogic techniques or ritual practices," notes a scholar, "but of God's grace and human cooperation with it."[23]

Unlike the other forms of yoga, Bhakti yoga invokes a religion of love and grace. No wonder, Indian scholars often describe Christianity as a "brilliant Bhakti highway" to God.

***

The legendary filmmaker James Cameron wrote and directed one of the highest-grossing films of all time, *Avatar*.[24] Not many people know that the word avatar comes straight from the theological dictionary of Hinduism. It originates from a Sanskrit word that literally means "to descend." In Hindu scriptures, an *avatar* represents the descent of God from the spiritual world into the material world.

This is exactly what the protagonist does in the movie *Avatar*. The paraplegic US marine Jake Sully enters the genetically engineered body of a "Navi" and lives among them on planet Pandora. Jake exists in two realities at the same time: his human body is inside a giant teleporter in the US camp, but his alien avatar lives in the Navi community.

In Christian lexicon, the word avatar is translated "incarnation." As a matter of fact, Christianity and Hinduism are the only two major religions that believe in the doctrine of incarnation. To picture God as human is sacrilegious for Jews and Muslims, and inconceivable for Buddhists and Sikhs. In most religious traditions, God is a transcendent entity who is never described in anthropomorphic terms. But in Christianity and in Hinduism, God is also immanent— He manifests Himself in a physical body. He can exist in both the finite and the infinite at the same time, just like Jake Sully in *Avatar*.

The most popular descents of Vishnu are collectively called *Dashavatar* or the "ten incarnations."[25] Rama and Krishna are the two most popular and commonly worshiped avatars in Hindu religion. A Hindu is encouraged to "live as Rama lived, learn what Krishna taught."[26]

Krishna is often depicted as a romantic figure, engaged in *rasalila* (love game) with his beloved Radha and her *gopis* (maids). Radha is Krishna's supreme beloved; she becomes one with him through pure love. Their relationship mirrors God's affinity to humanity: "The love of Radha and Krishna is symbolic of the eternal love affair between the devoted mortal and the Divine," says Swami Chinmayananda. "Radha's yearning for union with her beloved Krishna is the soul's longing for spiritual awakening to be united with the one Source of peace and bliss from which it has become separated."[27]

This romantic undertone in the relationship between the deity and the devotee in Bhakti yoga resonates deeply within the core theology of Christianity. The Bible, at times, portrays God as a "hopeless romantic," yearning for the love of His people. Jesus is a "bridegroom" who is betrothed to the church for the heavenly marriage to take place in the coming world.[28] In Hinduism and Christianity, therefore, religion is more of a romantic affair between the divine and the human than meticulous observance of rules and regulations.

The final avatar of Vishnu is Kalkin, the tenth and the last of the Dashavatar. Kalkin is the apocalyptic Messiah of Hinduism who will arrive at the end of this epoch (*Yuga*). The Hindu scriptures describe his impending appearance in vivid details, in a manner strikingly similar to that of the second coming of Jesus in the book of Revelation:

> At the end of Kali Yuga,
> when there exist no topics on the subject of God,
> even at the residences of so-called saints
> and respectable gentlemen,
> and when the power of government
> is transferred to the hands of
> ministers elected from the evil men,
> and when nothing is known of
> the techniques of sacrifice,
> the Lord will appear as
> the supreme chastiser.[29]

Kalkin is portrayed in Indian art as a king riding on a white horse with a silver sword in his hands. On the last day he will execute judgment on all creation. He will then reset the cosmic clock, announcing the birth of a new era. The *Kali Yuga* (Age of Vices) will end, and *Satya Yuga* (Age of Truth) will commence. As written in the book of Revelation, "I saw a new heaven and a new earth; for the first heaven and the first earth passed away.... Behold, I am making all things new."[30]

For Christians in India, the familiar concept of avatar presents itself as a term that aids in understanding the nature of Christ in relation to God. Indian theologians describe Jesus as the only avatar (Appasamy), the abiding avatar (Chakkarai), or the historical avatar (Griffiths).[31] Hindus would happily consider Jesus to be a perfect avatar, similar to Lord Krishna or Lord Kalkin, and give him an esteemed position in the Hindu pantheon. But for Christians, the uniqueness of Jesus Christ is of paramount importance. He is not one of many avatars; he is the only one.

There are many aspects in Jesus' life that will make him look like one of the avatars of Hinduism, yet there is an important one that distinguishes him from all the others—the purpose of incarnation. A Hindu avatar arrives in the world with a specific purpose:

> Whenever there is a decline in righteousness
> And an increase in unrighteousness,
> O Arjun, at that time I manifest myself on earth.
> To protect the righteous, to annihilate the wicked,
> And to reestablish the principles of dharma
> I appear on this earth, age after age.[32]

All avatars enter the world with one goal—to destroy the sinners and save the saints. Compare this to the purpose of the Christian avatar: "I did not come to call the righteous," said Jesus. "But sinners."[33]

Jesus descended from God with a diametrically different purpose than the rest of the avatars. "It is not those who are healthy who need a physician," said Jesus, "but those who are sick." He did not come to aid the righteous and destroy the sinners; rather, "the Son of Man has come to seek and to save that which was lost."[34]

Jesus, unlike the other avatars, was known to be a "friend of the sinners," not the saints. This is a matter of great comfort to many of us. If an avatar arrives to destroy the sinners, I will be one of the first to run for cover. If God came to this world looking for perfect people, I believe, he came to the wrong planet.

We come to realize that Jake Sully's story in *Avatar* finds its parallel in the Jesus story of the Bible. Sully came to planet Pandora proclaiming the imminent arrival of a different kingdom. He was commissioned to lead a military campaign against the Navi, but instead he strived to negotiate peace. In the end, the chastiser became the savior, and paid the ultimate price for salvation with his own life.

***

One of the fondest memories from my childhood is the celebration of Onam, a religious festival widely celebrated in the southern part of India. The story behind Onam fascinates me even today—unlike popular mythology, in this story, God plays the role of a villain.

Once upon a time, a king named Mahabali reigned over Kerala, the Indian state where I was born. This era was a golden age, where peace and prosperity prevailed in abundant measure. The lyrics of a popular folksong capture it in vivid details:

> When Mahabali ruled the land,
> All the people were regarded equal.
> They lived in the exuberance of joy
> Nothing could harm anyone.
> There was neither stress nor sickness,
> Children grew in complete health . . .

According to mythology, the gods who inhabited the heavenly world became jealous, and they conceived a devious plan to trick Mahabali. The Lord Vishnu appeared in the form of a dwarf (Vamana, one of the ten incarnations), and pleaded with the king to grant him three feet of land for performing a sacrifice ritual (yajna). The generous king happily obliged and granted him this modest wish.

The moment Mahabali made the promise, the unthinkable happened. Vamana's body grew into gigantic proportions and filled the universe. With one foot he measured the whole earth and with the next he measured the heavens. Now there was no place left to measure the third foot.

In order to honor his promise, Mahabali bowed his head so that Vamana could measure his third foot on his body. Vamana lowered his foot on the head of the king and pushed him all the way down into the netherworld. Mahabali's unwavering commitment to his promise pleased Vamana, however. So he granted the king permission to return to his kingdom once every year.

Onam is the day when the king returns from the underworld to visit his subjects.

What intrigues me the most in this story is the name of the king—Mahabali, which literally means "the great sacrifice."

The ritual of sacrifice is an all-pervasive sacrament in Hindu religion. Yajna (sacrifice) in itself is seen as the "very essence of the Vedas," says a Hindu doctrine. "From the early times, the ritual was understood to be the link between the human and the divine and a vehicle towards liberation."[35] Today blood sacrifices are not practical due to various governmental regulations that are set in place. Therefore, most Hindus have an altar in their house where they offer food, milk, and other gifts to their favorite deities.

Sacrifice is a central theme in the Hindu scriptures beginning from the creation story itself. According to the Vedas, the universe came into existence through the sacrifice of a deity, Prajapati (Lord of creatures), who appears as the creator god in the Rig Veda:

> O Prajapati, none other than thou encompasses all these creatures; for whatever object of desire we sacrifice to thee, let that be ours; may we be lords of riches.[36]

I remember visiting a temple dedicated to Prajapati in Northern India.[37] It looked more like an apartment building in the midst of a busy residential enclave. The hall was saturated with the aroma of burning incense. Melodic chants of sacred mantras filled the air. To my surprise, I found something that looked like an altar in the middle of the room, and a statue of Jesus placed on it.

"We are Hindus who worship Prajapati," said the priest. "We believe Jesus of Nazareth was the historical fulfillment of the Prajapati myth in Hinduism. He is the creator God who revealed Himself in history."

Conventional Christians in India view this Prajapati worship as a dangerous cult. However, as I dug deeper, the resemblances between Jesus and Prajapati became overwhelmingly obvious. One of the unique attributes of Prajapati, for example, is that he is half-human and half-divine. "Now, one half of that Prajapati was mortal, and the other half immortal," says the Upanishads. "With that part of him which was mortal he was afraid of death; and, being afraid, he became twofold, clay and water, and entered this [earth]."[38] This paradoxical combination of divinity and humanity is the first thing that comes to mind when I think of Jesus.

Prajapati is believed to be the one who established the ritual of sacrifice in order to commemorate a sacrifice he himself performed at the beginning of time, with his own body. The Rig Veda describes this Prajapati yajna, where Prajapati (also called Purusha, the primordial man) sacrificially dismembered his body to create the world.[39] "Prajapati is sacrifice," says an Upanishad. "For he created it in his own self-expression."[40]

A sacrifice may be performed for various reasons, whether to appease the gods or to atone for one's sins. But the true sacrifice is the Prajapati himself. "And indeed, there was no other victim meant for sacrifice but that one Prajapati. They did offer Him up. These were the first ordinances."[41]

The sacrifice of his own body did not kill Prajapati; it rather made him immortal. With his death the sacrificial man created life and returned to it.[42] "Prajapati became immortal; and in like manner does the Sacrificer become immortal by making that body [on the altar] immortal."[43]

The priest explained to me in great detail how different aspects of the Prajapati yajna were manifested in the crucifixion of Jesus Christ. He also quoted a Sanskrit scholar who affirms that the myth of Prajapati reflects the redemptive incarnation story of Jesus in the Bible.[44]

Jesus, like Prajapati, is the Lamb of God slain from the foundation of the world.[45] In Jesus, God presents Himself as the perfect and sufficient sacrifice for human iniquities. His death atones for our sins and restores our broken relationship with God. This is the true meaning of yajna.

In the Christian story, God metaphorically measures the heaven and the earth, only to encounter the infinite chasm that separates them. Jesus stands in the middle, bridging the gap between these divided worlds. He accepts the inevitable third foot, the measure of judgment, on himself and becomes the ultimate sacrifice (Mahabali). With his death he conquers death. With his sacrifice he produces eternal life. He is going to come back again to establish an eternal kingdom—a hope that sounds strikingly similar to that of Mahabali.

As a Christian journeying through Hinduism, I find both these religions occupying opposite ends of the theological spectrum—one is pantheistic, the other monotheistic; one fluid with many forms of worship and connections to God, the other seemingly dogmatic with only one way to Him. Yet, upon closer inspection, the faces of the savior figure emerging from them are not so far apart. In both religions, the infinite God enters the finite world as "Immanuel," the One who is with us. He performs the ultimate yajna for our redemption, and courts us into a (romantic) relationship with Him.

What if the God of the Bible, in His infinite grace, had chosen to reveal His descent into the world to my Hindu ancestors? I begin to wonder.

The Star of the Savior shines brighter even in the darkness that swoops on to overpower the light. The folk song of the religious festival Onam continues at a distance, reminiscing the glorious days of the great king:

No one said a lie,
There was no theft or deceit,
Measures and weights were right;
No one wronged his neighbor.
When Mahabali, ruled the land,
All the people were regarded equal.

Thy kingdom come, I pray.

3

THE SUFFERING SAVIOR

"I take upon myself the burden of all suffering . . .
At all costs I must bear the burdens of all beings. In that I do not follow
my own inclinations. I have made the vow to save all beings.
All beings I must set free."

Sikshasamuccaya, 280-81
(Vajradhvaja Sutra)[1]

*S*einfeld, a popular sitcom on American television, famously described itself as a "show about nothing." This phrase has since become a meme in popular culture, striking a deep chord of resonance with the futility of our collective search for the meaning of life.

In a segment titled "The Pitch," Jerry Seinfeld and George Costanza pitch a new television show to a group of studio executives.[2]

"I think I can sum up the show for you in one word," says George with a contemplative pause.

"Nothing."

"Nothing? What does it mean?" ask the befuddled executives.

"Nothing happens in the show, really. It is like life!"

As irreverent as *Seinfeld* itself might be, in curious ways this tagline mirrors the existential crisis at the very heart of the religion we call Buddhism.

As I started exploring this religion, the first thing that took me by surprise was the fact that the concept of God does not exist in it—neither the impersonal Brahman nor the personal Iswara. Isn't Buddha the God of Buddhism?, one might wonder. No, He is not. It turns out that we are all endowed with the Buddha nature, and all have the potential to become Buddha ourselves.

A religion without God does not make sense to me; yet it is nothing new to the culture in which I was born and raised. Most Eastern religions incorporate a healthy respect for agnosticism, and even atheism, within their wide spectrum of religious beliefs.

What is perplexing about Buddhism, to me, is its understanding of the personal soul, which, by the way, does not exist either. While Hinduism describes humans as embodied souls or *atman* (self), Buddhism considers us *anatman*, or "no-self." Our personality is "constantly changing" and "the idea of an immortal soul is simply an illusion that human beings impose on a process of constant change."[3]

"The individual has no real core," says Buddhism.[4] We are all nothing but a combination of cells, nerves, and blood, animated by our conscience. Identity is an illusion created by five components, *skandhas*—physical body, sensation, perception, cognition, and consciousness—that come together for a specific period of time. At the time of death, skandhas disperse into a "flux" and blend with other skandhas to form a new sentient being.[5]

In essence, our identity is similar to that of a car in which the mechanical components—the tires, brakes, engine, transmission system, and so on—come together to form an entity we perceive as a car. In reality all that exists are the components; the idea of a car in and of itself is an illusion.

To put it bluntly, life is a show about nothing.

Now perhaps you understand why Buddhism is growing rapidly in the Western world. It appeals to the scientific worldview of modernity, which portrays life as a compilation of atoms and molecules animated by a series of chemical rules. At the same time, it also plays into the spiritual sensibilities of postmodernity by offering us an opportunity to become "spiritual" without being "religious." In effect, you get the best of both worlds.

There is no God; there is no personal soul. All that really exists is "void" or emptiness.

This is why I consider Buddhism the *Seinfeld* of world religions—a show that deconstructs human life into a series of random acts, which eventually amounts to "nothing."

Is there more to Buddhism than this? Does it offer the potential to lead us to the personal God I see in the Bible or in other sacred scriptures? I would have to keep searching to find out.

***

Siddhartha Gautama was an Indian prince who lived in fifth-century BCE.[6] His father, King Suddhodana, was the ruler of Kapilavastu, which is part of modern-day Nepal.

Siddhartha married his cousin Yasodhara when they were both teenagers. The couple soon had a son, Rahula, who would be their only child.

Life seemed to be going well until one day when Siddhartha stepped outside the palace and came face to face with the harsh realities of a suffering world. The mortality of life and the meaninglessness of its existence haunted the prince. Leaving his wife and child behind, Siddhartha embarked on a spiritual journey. His goal was to find a solution to the problem of suffering.

Siddhartha was only twenty-nine years old when he left the palace. At first he joined a group of Hindu sadhus, who taught him Vedic philosophy and esoteric meditation techniques. After six years of intense ascetic life, he had a profound spiritual encounter, which came to be known as his "enlightenment." While meditating under a tree, Siddhartha came to the realization that the austerity of a monk is just as meaningless as the self-indulgence of a prince. The path to liberation, he concluded, is the "middle way"—a life which neither denies nor indulges in the pleasures of the world.

This realization awakened "the Buddha nature" in Siddhartha, and he came to be known as "the Buddha," or "the awakened one." Buddha then established the *sangha*, a community of monks dedicated to carrying his message of the middle way across the world. He continued his teaching for another four decades, and at age eighty, died of accidental food poisoning.

Buddha's solution to the problem of suffering is summarized in his teaching of the "four noble truths":

The first noble truth states the thesis, "All is suffering."

The second truth identifies the problem: "Desire is the root cause of suffering."

The third truth promises a solution: "Suffering has an end."

The fourth truth attempts to frame this solution in the form of an "eightfold path": "Right view, right resolve, right speech, right conduct, right occupation, right effort, right awareness, and right meditation."

As my journey took me deeper into the philosophy of Buddhism, I was disappointed to note that Buddha's solution to the problem of suffering is essentially an escape from the problem itself. None of his four noble truths offer, to my mind, a clear, workable solution to my own suffering.

The first truth is nothing but a restatement of the problem. The second truth essentially blames the victim. If I don't desire anything, I won't feel bad about the fact that I have nothing! A life without desire and passion leads to a suffering-free life, of course, but that wouldn't be life at all. The third truth is a default promise that every religion makes but most fail to deliver.

The eightfold path included in the fourth noble truth is certainly a noble way to live life, but I struggle to understand the word "right," which appears in all its eight propositions. If I do not believe in God, there is no absolute moral standard against which I can measure right or wrong. If everyone is left to decide what is right and wrong for themselves, the eightfold path, rather than eradicating suffering, will only become a perpetrator of it.

The more I looked at this religion, the more I came to believe that Buddha's core message of "the middle way" is nothing but commonsense advice, branded and packaged under the label of a religious philosophy. All that Buddha suggested was to follow a moderate lifestyle "in which the appetites were neither denied nor indulged to excess."[7] It is like a middle school counselor suggesting to her pupils that they should take half their courses in science and the other half in liberal arts, so that they can have a richer academic experience. It is certainly a noble counsel, but not a profound enough one on which we can build a religion.

In my view, Buddhism is essentially the story of the unraveling of one man's existential crisis and his journey in search of life's meaning. But what is the answer he found? I am not entirely sure.

***

The book of Ecclesiastes is undoubtedly the Biblical text that resonates the most with the core ideology of Buddhism. King Solomon, after setting his mind on seeking and exploring "all that has been done under heaven" comes to a devastating conclusion:

"Vanity of vanities," cries out Solomon. "Vanity of vanities! All is vanity."[8]

Buddhism ultimately brings us to the same conclusion. Consider the following exchange from a source that, while perhaps less profound than the Book of Ecclesiastes, still illuminates essential truths: *The Simpsons.*

In one of the episodes, Lisa Simpson walks into Springfield's Buddhist temple. Hollywood actor Richard Gere, a self-proclaimed Buddhist, is raking the Zen garden outside the temple. He gives Lisa a pamphlet that explains the basic precepts of Buddhism.

"All things are impermanent and empty of inherent existence," Lisa reads aloud. "Positive actions lead to happiness and negative actions lead to unhappiness." There is no better way to summarize Buddhism in less than ten seconds.

In a world with no God or individual souls, all that really exists is *shunya*, or emptiness. Even the ultimate liberation that Buddhism promises, *nirvana*, for all practical purposes, is nothing but a complete annihilation of life itself.

Buddhism subscribes to the reincarnation theory of Hinduism, but it does not clearly say what is actually being reincarnated. Hinduism has the concept of atman—a personal soul, the identity of which can be theoretically conceived. But a Buddhist anatman is not an individual soul, only a sentient energy which will eventually disappear into a psychic flux when the skandhas separate at the time of death. If that is the case, how does my karma follow me? Where am "I" anyway? Why should I care about what "I" do if the "I" itself does not exist?

Some suggest that the anatman being reincarnated is the "spiritual DNA" of a person. Others say it is the "moral identity" of an individual or "the mind stream" of his or her conscience. Whatever word games you choose to play, the law of karma cannot operate without an individual soul taking moral responsibility for each action performed in a life cycle.

The problem becomes even more serious at the end of the reincarnation cycle where the sentient being achieves "nirvana." What is nirvana? It is a mode of existence very similar to moksha in Hinduism, where the atman becomes one with Brahman. But what does nirvana look like in a Buddhist universe where there is no atman or Brahman?

Once again, pundits come up with different explanations for the term nirvana. It is "a kind of gnosis, or direct apprehension of truth, which deepens over time and eventually reaches full maturity in the complete awakening experienced by the Buddha," says one Buddhist scholar.[9] It is a "fusion of virtue and wisdom," says another. Yet another scholar describes it as a "transformed state of personality characterized by peace, deep spiritual joy, compassion and a refined and subtle awareness."[10] As profound as these explanations seem to appear, they are nothing but crafty words of accomplished wordsmiths. It means very little to someone who is actually suffering from an existential crisis.

As a matter of fact, Buddha himself was unable to answer questions on the true nature of nirvana. He told his disciples that only those who experience nirvana could really understand what it is. Instead of trying to speculate what nirvana is, he said, they should strive to achieve it.

Nirvana might be perceived as a state of pure bliss. Yet in reality, it is nothing but pure emptiness or shunya.

This concept of nothingness also happens to be at the very center of the Buddhist solution to the problem of suffering. The experience of suffering is not real, says Buddhism. It is an illusion. The only solution to our existential crisis is to withdraw from the perceived physical reality and transcend into the world of emptiness.

I have to say that I find this solution both unhelpful and, in some cases, irresponsible. It offers the sufferer no relief. A rape victim, for example, has to convince herself that the emotional and physical pain inflicted on her by the perpetrator is nothing but an illusion. A single mother has to tell her starving children that the hunger they are experiencing is "unreal"; perhaps their little tummies are being filled in an alternate version of reality.

Also troubling to me is the fact that Buddhism uses the theory of reincarnation to explain the problem of suffering. All those who suffer in the world, according to the law of karma, are suffering because of the bad karma they accumulated from their previous lives. They deserve what they are going through; their misery is of their own making.

In my opinion this is nothing but a cowardly attempt to escape from the actual problem, once again, using the infamous strategy, "blaming the victim." If we were to subscribe to this explanation, we will also have to believe that the thousands of souls who were trapped in the World Trade center on 9/11 happened to be there because of the many atrocities they had committed in their previous lives. The six million Jews mercilessly butchered during the Holocaust, according to this theory, must have been some kind of notorious thugs in their previous lives. This is no solution to suffering; it is rather a dangerous attempt to rationalize and perpetuate suffering.[11]

As far as I am concerned, all that the reincarnation theory does is justifying the status quo. It does not challenge us to take any action to relieve our neighbor's suffering. After all, the sufferer is suffering because of his or her own bad karma.

The theory of emptiness in Buddhism leads us to a nihilist worldview, pushing humanity to the brink of a moral abyss. The theory of vanity in the book of Ecclesiastes, in contrast, ends on a completely different note. "The conclusion, when all has been heard, is: fear God and keep His command-ments, because this applies to every person," says Ecclesiastes. "For God will bring every act to judgment, everything which is hidden, whether it is good or evil."[12]

Prince Siddhartha and King Solomon made the same observations, but they arrived at dramatically different conclusions. To one, nothing matters; to the other, everything does.

Rob Johnston, professor of theology and culture at Fuller Seminary, uses the book of Ecclesiastes as a lens to interpret the elements of redemptive revelations in modern cinema. He often states an aphorism in the class, which summarizes the message of the book beautifully:

"Life sucks, but it is wonder-filled."

Life in Siddhartha's world sucks because it is empty and void. The life in Solomon's world also sucks; yet the presence of God instills it with beauty and meaning.

***

I never had an opportunity to meet a Buddhist while I lived in India. I think one has a better chance of running into a suit-wearing Mormon missionary in India than a saffron-wearing Buddhist monk.

It is a cold irony that a religion that has spread its wings and flown across the world has become an endangered species in its birthplace. Why would a country that holds no bars against any religion turn its back on one of its own?

This point is of particular interest considering the fact that Buddhism is, and always has been, a missionary religion. Buddha travelled across India as an itinerant missionary, covering an area of approximately 37,500 square miles (as opposed to roughly 5,000 square miles by Jesus). Buddha taught his message over a span of forty years (as opposed to less than four years in the case of Jesus). On his deathbed, Buddha commissioned sixty elders to propagate his message across the world (as opposed to the twelve apostles of Jesus).

Buddhism had the added glamour of being a religion founded by a prince, especially at a time when the priestly class controlled most other religions. The priestly religions were in constant tension with the "emperor cults" in Asian countries. The rulers found it easy to embrace a religion founded by one of their own. Emperor Ashoka, for example, declared Buddhism to be India's state religion and sent out thousands of Buddhist missionaries across the world.[13]

The people of India, however, rejected Buddhism simply because it had nothing new to offer to their already saturated religious souls. The highly touted Buddhist philosophy, as far as the Hindus are concerned, is just a remix of their own philosophical propositions. So when Buddha's disciples went around preaching the middle way, Indians saw the new religion as nothing but "Hinduism Lite." As one of my Hindu friends says, "If Buddha claims to have established a new religion, Hindus will file for copyright infringement."

Buddhist missionaries soon left India and travelled northward to China, Korea, and Japan. The people of these countries welcomed them, assuming that they were Hindu monks from India. The predominant religions in this region at the time were Confucianism and Taoism. Confucianism was a set of socio-ethical principles and Taoism a way to live in harmony with nature; neither had much to say about gods or afterlife. The people of Asia expected Buddhist missionaries to bring them an unlimited supply of gods and goddesses from Hinduism.

The monks exploited this opportunity and devised a "folk version" of Buddhism, tailor-made to the needs of the god-starved masses of Asia. In order to outshine humanistic Confucianism and mystical Taoism, they imported magic and mantras from Hinduism. Although Buddhist doctrines affirmed there was no God, the missionaries borrowed as many gods and goddesses as they could from the Hindu pantheon. They encouraged the devotees to worship Buddha as God Himself, and the other deities as his various manifestations.[14]

Buddhism adopted the same strategy even as it entered the West. Individualism and scientific rationalism were the dominant ideologies of the time; so the missionaries incorporated self-help theories and empowerment ideologies to their doctrines. As a scholar wisely noted, "the fact that Buddhism imposes few confessional, ritual or other requirements on its followers makes it easy to live as a Buddhist in a pluralistic milieu and minimizes the likelihood of overt conflict with secular values."[15]

A religion that started as a reformed version of Hinduism in the East thus became a baptized version of scientific humanism in the West.[16]

The new and improved version of Buddhism in the West is an esoteric mix of atheism and New Age spirituality. "Buddhism teaches the way to perfect goodness and wisdom without a personal God; the highest knowledge without a revelation ... the possibility of redemption without a vicarious redeemer," says a Buddhist monk. It is "a salvation in which everyone is his own savior."[17] Why do we need God if we can design our own salvation? Why surrender to Him if we can be the masters of our own destiny? What a tempting offer!

***

I sat on a wooden bench in the Deer Park at Saranath, a city in the northern part of India. Although Buddha was born in Kapilavasthu, Buddhism was born here in Saranath. This is where Buddha preached his first sermon, laying out the four noble truths.

I had a clear view of the *Dhamekh Stupa*, a cylindrical coffin in which Buddha's remains rest. A group of barefooted monks walked around it chanting *dharma sutras*. The visitors, mostly tourists from other South Asian countries, marched behind them. Some of them kissed the Stupa and sprinkled it with incenses and flower petals. The prayers they muttered were choked in tears.

The Buddhism I saw in Saranath was quite different from the Buddhism I learned from watching *The Simpsons*. The Buddhists I saw there were like followers of any other religion. They were passionate devotees of a transcendent deity. They believed in god(s), and they were certainly concerned about their personal soul.

This is what "real" Buddhism looks like in most parts of the world. Although Western Buddhism claims to be a religion without God, the Buddhists in the rest of the world know that no religion can survive without a god. A religion without God can be a great topic for the coffee table conversations of intellectual elites, but it will have no power to address the "felt needs" of ordinary people.

Indeed, what we know of Buddhism from the Western media is a far cry from what is often practiced in Buddhist temples across the world. Buddhism is considered pantheistic in the majority world, as most Buddhists worship gods, and some even demons. The monks function as priests, exercising ecclesiastical authority over congregations. As a Buddhist scholar observes, "Buddhists have familiar patterns of ritual and worship. They go on pilgrimages to important shrines; they worship images and sites that are sacred to Buddha; and they mark the stages of life with rites of passage."[18]

Ordinary Buddhists do not care much about nirvana; they rather hope for an afterlife free of suffering, reunited with their loved ones. Japanese Buddhists, for example, imagine a celestial paradise, "Pure Land," where gods and goddesses reside. This paradise is described in material terms, and its description closely resembles the "new heaven" described in the book of Revelation:

> Land of Ultimate Bliss is everywhere surrounded by seven tiers of railings, seven layers of netting, and seven rows of trees, all formed from the four treasures. . . . It has pools of the seven jewels, filled with the eight waters of merit and virtue. . . . On the four sides are stairs of gold, silver, lapis lazuli, and crystal; above are raised pavilions adorned with gold, silver, lapis lazuli, crystal, mother-of-pearl, red pearls, and carnelian. In the pools are lotuses as large as carriage wheels. . . . In that Buddha land there is always heavenly music . . . there are always rare and wonderful varicolored birds. . . . In the six periods of the day and night the flocks of birds sing forth harmonious and elegant sounds . . . Those living beings who hear should vow, "I

wish to be born in that country." And why? Those who thus attain are all superior and good people, all coming together in one place.[19]

In the same vein, there are also multiple levels of "hell" in Buddhism. There are cold hells where people are tortured by freezing, and hot hells where they are roasted in fire. The only good news about the Buddhist hell is that it is not a place of eternal damnation. People will be released from hell once they finish paying for all their bad karma. A Western Buddhist may consider these beliefs to be superstitious, but it is the only type of Buddhism that has stood the test of time.

There are no unified codes or central authority figures in Buddhism. The Dalai Lama is often considered the spokesperson of Buddhism in the West, but in reality, he represents only a small sect of Buddhists who are part of the Vajrayana (diamond vehicle) tradition that incorporates many esoteric rituals and psychic experiments from other religious traditions into Buddhist practice. Although he presents himself as a charismatic monk in popular media, in reality, the Dalai Lama represents an occult religion that borrows from tantric Hinduism and Tibetan shamanism. He is revered in Tibet as the manifestation of a celestial Buddha, whose title is passed on from one life to the next through the reincarnation cycle.[20]

There are, of course, many schools of teaching in Buddhism. They emerged out of the schisms that sprung up in the community immediately after Buddha's death. In a council that met not long after his passing, the sangha split into Theravada (doctrine of elders), a conservative faction that stuck to the original teachings of Buddha; and Mahayana (great vehicle), a liberal wing, which argued that the only way for survival was to adapt to the traditions of indigenous religions.

Theravada still claims an unbroken lineage of monks that extends all the way back to Buddha. Mahayana, on the other hand, de-emphasizes the historical Buddha and argues that all aspirants will become Buddhas at some point in time.

A few American Buddhists are now calling for a "*Navayana*" (new vehicle) Buddhism, one that "blends with the best of Western science, psychology and social science... Its forms must ever change to serve the ever-changing human need."[21] It is this adeptness to adaptability that makes Buddhism one of the most favored religions in the West.

***

The Matrix, the 1999 blockbuster directed by the Wachowski brothers, was a benchmark film that set new standards for style and storytelling in Hollywood. One of the unique attributes of the film that many critics gravitated towards was its philosophical undertone. The story of *The Matrix* resonated with the spiritual sensibilities of the viewers. Some even described watching the film as an "enlightening" experience.

The story of *The Matrix* has interesting parallels to the Buddhist narrative of the universe. The film suggests that we live in a virtual world—what we see with our eyes and hear with our ears exists only in our imagination. It is an illusion created by an artificial intelligence. Consider the similarities to the Buddhist world, where we are imprisoned within an illusory matrix created by our own karmic impressions.

The hero of *The Matrix* is a computer hacker named Neo, who manages to break through the walls of the matrix and enter the realm of reality. This is what liberation looks like in Buddhism. A true Buddha leaps over the walls of the samsara cycle and enters the realm of nirvana.

The Matrix does not stop with liberation, however. Neo comes back to the matrix as an enlightened savior. He is the fulfillment of a prophecy. He is the One they have been waiting for!

Is there such a savior figure in Buddhism? Apparently the answer is yes. This savior figure is called a *bodhisattva*.

The bodhisattva, like Neo, attains nirvana but chooses to come back to the samsara instead of remaining in the realm of nirvana. He continues in the reincarnation cycle without passing into absolute Buddhahood. He will become Buddha only when his mission on earth is accomplished.

A bodhisattva, therefore, is a "Buddha-to-be." All Bodhisattvas will one day become Buddha. Until then they postpone their own nirvana in order to help others achieve enlightenment. They are, therefore, the ultimate symbol of compassion, which is the supreme virtue in Buddhism.

Bodhisattvas possess superhuman abilities to switch between their appearances. They can also travel between the heavenly and the earthly realms. Each time they reach heaven, however, the bodhisattvas decide to return to the world for the sake of others. This mission requires great suffering and sacrifice on their part.[22]

Siddhartha is believed to be one such bodhisattva who came back from nirvana to teach us what we now know as Buddhism. "Although the historical Buddha had appeared to live and die like an ordinary man, he had, in reality, been enlightened from time immemorial," notes a scholar. "As a wise and compassionate teacher, however, he had gone through an elaborate charade to accommodate the expectations of the people of the time."[23]

Today bodhisattvas have become the Buddhist equivalent of Hindu gods. According to scholars, "the cult of bodhisattvas . . . promised not just rebirth in another world, but in direct assistance with the concern of this life, such as the birth of a child or prosperity in the family."[24] Worshippers picture them as celestial beings with mythological attributes or as human beings with supernatural powers. They are venerated as local deities in their devotional cult.

The bodhisattva who is more popular in Japan is Amida/Amidaba (Buddha of Infinite Light), the custodian of Pure Land. Those who have enough good karma can choose to be reborn into this paradise instead of entering nirvana. In Pure Land they also have the option to go back to the earthly realm in order to become bodhisattvas.

Another bodhisattva, named Avalokitesvara (the Lord Who Looks Down), is worshipped in Tibet and China. Tibetans believe that the Dalai Lama is the reincarnation of Avalokitesvara. The Chinese, on the other hand, consider Avalokitesvara to be female, and worship her as a white-robed deity, Guan-yin (One Who Hears the Sound).

Perhaps the most popular bodhisattva in the west is the laughing Buddha (Hoeti), also known as Maitreya. He lives in a paradise called "Tushita" (pleasurable), from where he will return at the end of this age. He will establish "a utopian era in which multitudes will gain enlightenment."[25]

In South Asia many have formed "messianic" cults in the name of Maitreya, proclaiming the arrival of the Buddha era.

An intriguing aspect of the bodhisattva ideology is its emphasis on "grace" as the primary means to achieve liberation. Francis Xavier, an early Roman Catholic missionary to Japan,[26] famously described Buddhism as a "Lutheran heresy," because it preached salvation by grace alone, not by human effort.[27] Japanese Buddhists believe that Amidaba Buddha will take anyone who chants "Namu Amida Butsu" (Praise Amida Buddha) to Pure Land. "It was no longer possible to rely on one's own efforts to achieve salvation," said Honen, one of the Buddhist teachers of the medieval era.[28] "The only way to be saved is simply to trust the grace of Amida Buddha."[29]

I have come across many Buddhists who believe Jesus was one of the many bodhisattvas who has taken the vow "to work tirelessly over countless lifetimes to lead others to nirvana."[30] As bodhisattvas exist in both samsara and nirvana at the same time, Jesus is simultaneously present in the life of a believer and at the right hand of "the Father." His teachings reflect many Buddhist ideals, and his cross represents the epitome of Buddhist virtues.

Taking of the bodhisattva vow is an important ritual in Mahayana Buddhism. I remember watching one such ceremony in Los Angeles. A group of initiates from different age groups and ethnic makeups sat cross-legged and close-eyed, repeating after a teacher who officiated the ceremony:

> However innumerable all beings are,
> I vow to save them all.

However inexhaustible my delusions are,
I vow to overcome them all.
However immeasurable the teachings are,
I vow to fathom them all. [31]

The "real" Buddhism, like most other religions, has its own gods and goddesses. "How can a tradition that placed so much emphasis on self-reliance be transformed into a tradition of reliance on celestial or other worldly savior?" laments a scholar.[32] The answer is surprisingly simple. No religion can survive without a god.

People choose religion not only to learn the right way, but also to find the strength to walk in it. The eightfold path might show us a noble way to live our life, but the problem is that we are humanly incapable of living it. What we really need, therefore, is not another teacher who can theorize the problem of suffering, but a savior who can actually redeem us in the midst of it.

A teacher shows us the way, but a savior becomes the way.

I stand at the crossroad, looking for a bodhisattva who can save me. The road is dark and narrow. But the Star of the Savior is still shining from the northern sky.

The journey continues.

THE WORD BECOMES THE LORD

*"The Shabad [Word] is the Guru, upon whom
I lovingly focus my consciousness;
I am the disciple."*

Guru Granth Sahib 943-1, 68 /44

It was four days after 9/11. Balbir Singh Sodhi, an immigrant from India, walked out of the gas station he owned in Mesa, Arizona. He was in his traditional Sikh attire: a turban on his head and his long beard neatly combed and tucked inside it.

A Chevrolet truck drove up to him. A .38 caliber handgun peered through the window. It spit out five bullets.

The gunman screamed, "All you towelheads, go home!"

Balbir Singh Sodhi died on the spot. He was the first of the many Sikh casualties in a series of hate crimes that erupted in the US in the wake of 9/11. Less than a month later, a group of teenagers would burn down a Sikh temple in New

York, claiming it was named after Osama bin Laden. Another gunman would go on a shooting rampage in a Sikh temple in Wisconsin, killing six people and wounding many others.

Unfortunately, Sikhs were the "unintentional victims" in these tragic acts of violence. The perpetrators got them confused with Islamic jihadists because they looked a lot like the terrorists shown on the television screens. The Sikhs are wrongfully associated with Islam even today, primarily on account of their religious attire.

There is an ugly irony in this case: Islam is the religion that has persecuted Sikhism the most in the past five centuries of its existence.[1] But the Sikhs are now victimized once again for the atrocities allegedly committed by their tormentors.

Why would Sikhs follow a dress code that makes them look like Muslims? We need to go back to the origins of their religion to answer this question.

Sikhism was born in India out of a cultural marriage between Hinduism and Islam in the fifteenth century. Guru Nanak, the founder of Sikhism, was a Hindu who was significantly influenced by the religious worldview of his Muslim teacher. He was born in Punjab, a region now split between India and Pakistan. He got married at the age of twelve, had two sons, and lived a normal life as a civil servant until he turned thirty.

Around this time, Nanak had a profound spiritual encounter. It happened while he was taking bath in a river. As the story goes, he remained in the river for three days, receiving a series of revelations from God. The God who appeared to Nanak had no name. Therefore Nanak called

Him *Sat Nam*, or the True Name.[2] The message Sat Nam revealed to him is encapsulated in a single phrase: "There is neither Hindu nor Muslim."

Following this spiritual encounter, Guru Nanak chose to wear an outfit that symbolized this message: half-Muslim (i.e. the turban on the head) and half-Hindu (i.e. the tunic of a holy man). Even today all the males "initiated"[3] into the religion follow this dress code, often identified by the "5 Ks":

Kesh: Uncut hair and beard, tucked inside the turban.
Kansha: A comb for grooming the hair and the beard.
Kirpan: A small dagger used for self-defense.
Karha: A bracelet worn on the right hand, like a military dog tag.
Kacha: Long shorts, an undergarment usually worn by soldiers.

What Guru Nanak taught is a hybrid religion that evolved out of Hinduism and Islam. Sat Nam, like the Allah of Islam, is a transcendent entity who cannot be described in human terms. The *mul mantra*, the opening verse of the Sikh sacred scripture and a daily prayer of the Sikhs, resembles closely to the Islamic *shahada*:

There is but one God. He is True Name, the Creator. He is devoid of fear and enmity. He is unborn, immortal and self-existent. By the grace of Guru He is obtained.

The cosmology of the Sikh religion, however, finds its roots in Hinduism. A soul transmigrates from one life to the other through different species in the reincarnation cycle. In the end it receives *mukti*—a blissful union with God (unlike moksha of Hinduism where we become one with the impersonal Absolute, or nirvana of Buddhism where we dissolve into emptiness). This alternate reality, *sachkhand*, is a paradise where we get to reunite with our loved ones while also enjoying the utmost intimacy with God.[4]

Guru Nanak travelled the country preaching this revelation, and those who followed him were called the *sikhs* (disciples). Today Sikhism is the fifth-largest religion in the world, with over twenty-five million followers.[5]

***

Geographically speaking, Punjab, the Sikh territory, and Kerala, my home state, are situated in the northern and the southern borders of India. I never had the opportunity to befriend a Sikh while I lived in the country. As a matter of fact, the first Sikh I ever met was in a church in Canada; she has since become a good friend and colleague.

Mona was born and raised in an orthodox Sikh family in India. One day she attended a Christian youth camp with one of her friends. She was introduced to the teachings of Jesus, which, at first, sounded remarkably similar to that of her own religion. After all, Sikhism encourages its followers to respect all teachers who offer a path to enlightenment.

Sikhism is a religion of teachers, or the Gurus. A Sikh temple is called *Gurdwara*, or the house of the Guru. In addition to the founder, Guru Nanak, there have been nine other Gurus in the Sikh lineage.[6] The tenth Guru, Guru Gobind Singh, took *Adi Granth*, the sacred text of Sikhism, and designated it as the last and the eternal Guru. The Sikhs now revere their scripture as *Guru Granth Sahib*, the Word (or Book) Guru, and treat it as a living person. As we will discuss later, this idea of the "living word" resembles closely to the "Word becoming flesh" theology of Christianity.

In the Sikh cosmology the ten Gurus are like ten candles lit by the same flame. Above them is the Sat Guru, the True Teacher, who is God Himself. The Sat Guru is the flame that enlightens the Gurus, and through them, the rest of the world. As Guru Granth Sahib puts it,

> My Supreme Guru has created everything.
> I perform devotional worship service to You,
> And fall at Your Feet, O Lord.[7]

The Sat Guru, according to Sikhism, is the creator of the world. He reveals the truth about God to the world through His Word. He is also the giver of peace to humanity and is the only hope of our salvation.[8]

As Mona started reading the Bible, she found the depiction of Jesus eerily similar to that of the Sat Guru in Guru Granth Sahib. Jesus (as *logos*) is the creator of the world; he offers us peace; he is the one through whom salvation can be received. Above all, Jesus reveals God to humanity and leads us into spiritual union with Him.[9] Mona instinctively knew that the Jesus of the Bible was the historical manifestation of the mythical Sat Guru, spoken of in the Guru Granth Sahib.

She also realized that the Sikh Gurus revered Jesus as pure and unique. One such reference was found in Guru Arjan's book, *Sukhmani*, where Jesus is described as someone who "cut off the head of *Rakhshus* [devil]. He is holy and unique Isa [Jesus] of the world. . . . He is holy and unique and for the whole world."[10]

As Mona continued to study both religions side by side, it seemed to her that "where Sikhism lacked answers, Christianity filled the gaps." As a musician, she was particularly fascinated by the way in which the language of love and grace, characteristic to Sikh hymns, is reflected in Christian songs. The lyrics of the Guru Granth Sahib express "the devotee's condition: his aspirations and yearning, his agony in separation and his longing to be with the Lord."[11] In the same way Christianity also portrays the relationship between God and humans in romantic terms, often depicting Christ as a groom and we as his bride.[12]

"Grace is a word that appears in both Christian and Sikh scriptures referring to the undeserved gift of God," posits Mona. "The Sikhs, like Christians, believe in a loving God who gives us grace (prasad) in our spiritual journey." The Sikhs, however, do not view grace as the only means to salvation. It is part of God's response to an individual's acts of meditation and charity. In Christianity, grace is an absolute. "There is no other way to receive salvation," says Mona. "We did nothing to deserve it. I did nothing to deserve it. All that was required of me [to become a Christian] was to respond in faith."

The moment of "enlightenment" Mona had at the youth camp eventually redirected her personal spiritual journey in a completely different direction.[13] Today she is an ordained minister with the Presbyterian Church of Canada and a noted conference speaker, appearing on numerous stages and in television programs. As I am writing this, she is working on her PhD in theology at one of the most prestigious universities in Canada.

Mona's encounter with Jesus Christ may have been unique, but most Sikhs share similar sentiments when it comes to his stature as a Guru. When the BBC asked a selected group of Sikhs to share their opinion about Jesus, Nikki Singh wrote: "Though I may not see him as one of the Ten Sikh Gurus, he is a distinct and vital parallel who continues to play a very significant role in my life as a Sikh ... Jesus has been a wonderful mirror who in his unique form and vocabulary promoted my self-understanding."[14]

***

The Golden Temple in Amritsar, Punjab, is an architectural marvel of India, second only to the Taj Mahal. Constructed by the fifth Guru Arjan Singh in 1601, this Gurdwara is considered the religious center of Sikhism.

The memory of my visit to the Golden Temple is colored with its sublime beauty and tranquility. The golden dome, built according to the conventions of Islamic architecture, glitters in the bright sunlight, proclaiming the majesty of God. The towering steeples on the four gates, inspired by Hindu architecture, invite people from all four corners of the world to worship Him.

The first thing I noticed in the Gurdwara was its muted interiors. I was surprised to see how simple and plain the sanctuary appeared in contrast to its ostentatious exterior. There were no idols or sacred images, no one performing elaborate rituals or ceremonies. All kinds of idols and religious rituals are prohibited in Sikhism.

The focus of worship in a Gurdwara is the Guru Granth Sahib, the sacred scripture of Sikhism. In order to turn to God, Sikhs believe that one must listen to *gurbani*, the singing of devotional songs from the scripture. It is believed that the repeated reading of the scripture accelerates one's journey to salvation.[15] A typical service consists of devotees singing hymns and presenting their offerings in front of the Guru Granth Sahib.

The Guru Granth Sahib, like the Quran, is so revered that any translation from the original "*Gurumukhi*" script makes it inauthentic. What intrigues me the most is the name of the scripture itself. The word *sahib* means the "Lord"—a reverential title attributed only to a person. Imagine Christians calling their scripture "Mr. Bible" or Muslims addressing their scripture as "Sir Quran"!

The Sikh devotion to their scripture and their treatment of it as a living, breathing person is by far one of the most unique things I have seen in any religion. Guru Granth Sahib is "roused" every morning, carried on top of a devotee's head, draped in fine silk, and kept on a throne under a canopy. When it is being read, a whisk is waved over it like a fan, as if to cool it from exhaustion. At the end of the day, it is put to rest in a special chamber covered with ornate blankets. In orthodox Sikh families, Sahib will have "his" own special bedroom like any other member of the family.

My friend Mona recalled how each morning her mother would go into her *Babaji* room, where the Guru Granth Sahib "lived" in their home. "The holy book was on a small table dressed with beautiful silks and brocades. I would sit on the floor in front while my mother conducted the morning ritual of opening the holy book. She would read a passage... and conclude by saying the *japji*, the morning prayer. Every morning began this way and every evening, before sundown, this was repeated when the holy book was closed."

In theory Sikhism forbids any portrayal of God in the form of a person. "Let that mouth be burnt, which says that our Lord and Master is subject to birth," says the scripture. "He is not born, and He does not die; He does not come and go in reincarnation."[16] Any individual who has taken birth in this world, including the Sikh Gurus, cannot be considered a direct manifestation of God.

Sikhs, however, believe that God makes Himself known to us through His *shabad* (Word). The Word is therefore the true Guru. He lives among us to show the way. In fact, He Himself is the way. As Guru Nanak wrote, "the shabad is the Guru, upon whom I lovingly focus my consciousness; I am the disciple."[17]

It is practically impossible to overlook the striking similarity between the Sikh understanding of the Guru Granth Sahib and the Christian conception of Jesus as the incarnate Word of God. The way Sikhism attributes personality to their scripture brings to mind the Christian understanding of the Word coming down in human flesh to dwell among us.[18] When John introduced Jesus to the world, he borrowed a loaded term from the Greek philosophy—*logos*, which is translated "the Word." Word is a tangible expression of the mind; therefore logos represents the mind of God—a life source that possesses will, intellect, and emotions. In other words, logos is the very essence of God.

"In the beginning was the logos," says John. "The logos was with God and the logos was God."[19] The logos descended into the human world with a divine mission. His first mission was the creation of the world, where His action was clearly manifested, but His person was hidden. In the next mission, however, we get to see both His action and His person. "The logos became flesh, and dwelt among us," continues John. "And we saw His glory, glory as of the only begotten from the Father, full of grace and truth."[20] The logos became a man.

The world saw the Word in the person of Jesus Christ. In him, the shabad (Word) became the sahib (Lord).

I am beginning to think that the path being lit by the Star of the Savior is not as narrow or singular as I once believed it to be. Could the Wise Men hear the heartbeats of the Sat Guru, pulsating within the pages of the Guru Granth Sahib?

Get closer. Listen with your heart.

5

THE MAN WHO BECAME A SIGN

"She said: "How shall I have a son, seeing that no man has touched me, and I am not unchaste?" He said: "So (it will be): Thy Lord saith, 'That is easy for Me: and (We wish) to appoint him as a Sign unto men and a mercy from Us.'"

Al Quran (Sura 19:21)

The first thing Abdul Rahman did as he entered the dorm was build a makeshift shrine on his table.

He pulled out a thick, leather-bound book and gently placed it in the shrine. He closed his eyes for a quick second and lowered his head. There was a reverential silence.

It was my second year at the Mahatma Gandhi University in India. Abdul and I were randomly matched as roommates in the college dorm. In the four years that followed, we became close friends and confidants.

The book Abdul placed on the easel was the Quran, the sacred text of Islam.

Despite his worshipful attitude towards the Quran, Abdul rarely read the book. He did not have to. He had memorized most of it, and he could chant many verses on command. He did so in fluent Arabic, with the original intonation.

It took me a while to realize that Abdul did not know the meaning of these verses that incessantly flowed out of his mouth. Like any other Muslim boy, he had received the formal training to read the Quran in a *madrasa*, the religious school for Muslims. He only had to know enough Arabic to be able to recite the verses; learning the vocabulary was not important. A pious Muslim considers the recitation of the Quranic verses, whether one understands its meaning or not, a noble act in itself. In fact, interpretation of the meaning is a job strictly confined within the domain of the clergy.

It is a foundational belief in Islam that the Quran must exist only in Arabic. The official readings of the Quran are done only in that language. There are no "authorized versions" in other languages, and translation is permitted only if it is accompanied by the original Arabic text. My roommate Abdul's Quran, for example, was in Arabic, but each verse was paired with a translation in Malayalam, our mother tongue. He did not care much for the local language version, because he believed, as many Muslims do, that the very act of translation corrupts the Quran.

Abdul believed that his God, Allah, is the same God as that of the Jews and the Christians. Allah is the one who revealed the "Old" Testament (*Torah*) to Moses and the "New" Testament (*Injil*) to Jesus. But the Jews angered Him by killing His prophets, and the Christians blasphemed His name by making Him part of a "Trinity."[1] Therefore Allah sent the Quran, the uncorrupted revelation, through

Muhammad. The Quran, being the latest and the final revelation, supersedes the Jewish Torah and the Christian Injil.

The Quran in Abdul's shrine was not as voluminous as it appeared to be. In reality, it was much shorter than my Bible—even smaller than the New Testament.[2] It only appeared large because of the size of the Arabic calligraphy.

As a truth-seeker, I was intrigued by Abdul's faith, and fascinated by his reverence for this sacred text. After much pleading and a lot of persuasion, Abdul allowed me to read his Quran. There was one condition, however: I had to take a shower each time before I touched the book. As unpleasant as it was for any teenager, I yielded grudgingly. In retrospect, I gratefully acknowledge that the enforcement of this rule kept me in good hygiene during my university years.

***

Islam is the second-largest religion in the world with over 1.6 billion adherents as I write this book.

It is considered a minority religion in India, but the Muslims in India far outnumber the Muslims in Iran, Iraq, and Saudi Arabia combined.

Islam is an integral part of India's cultural heritage. Not many people know that the Taj Mahal, the iconic marble mausoleum that has become India's defining cultural icon, is a contribution of Islamic architecture.

As a matter of fact, Islam was born just on the other side of the Arabic ocean that borders India on the west. It happened roughly 1,400 years ago. The Arabian Peninsula at the time was the battleground between two political superpowers—the Byzantine Empire in the West and the Persian Empire in the East. The region was inhabited by various nomadic tribes who had no organized social structure or religion. The only place they came together was at Mecca, a city which is today in Saudi Arabia. Once every year, all the Arabs gathered in the same place to offer sacrifices to their gods and goddesses. There were roughly 360 deities housed inside a cube-shaped temple called the *Kaba*, each of them representing the various local tribes and their diverse religious practices.

In the seventh century CE, a prophetic figure appeared on the scene. He claimed he had a divine mandate to unify the Arab tribes against the invading powers of Byzantine and Persian empires. His name was Muhammad.

Muhammad was neither statesman nor scholar. He was rather an *ammi*, a person with little formal education, and a caravan trader by profession. His parents had died soon after he was born.[3] His uncle Abu Talib introduced his young nephew to the caravan business. Muhammad excelled at the trade, and his employer, a widow named Khadija, began to take notice. She fell for his youthful charm and soon decided to marry him. She was forty and he was only twenty-five. The alliance, however, brought Muhammad wealth, social status, and political power.

Over time, Muhammad realized that the real cause of division among the Arabs was not tribal politics, but religion. The best way to unify the people, he believed, was to get rid of all the gods and goddesses (*ilahs*) that separated them, and to bring the nation together under "the God" (*Al ilah*).

One day, when he was around the age of forty, Muhammad had a visitation from angel Gabriel. He enlightened him with a series of revelations from this one God, Allah. As the story goes, Muhammad heard the majestic voice of the angel reverberating in the clefts of Mount Hera:

> Recite in the name of your Lord who created,
> Created man from a clinging substance.
> Recite, and your Lord is the most Generous,
> Who taught by the pen,
> Taught man that which he knew not.[4]

The first word Muhammad heard, "*Iqra*," (Quran: recite) became the title of a series of revelations that he continued to receive until his death. Being an ammi, Muhammad did not write down these revelations meticulously. Instead he memorized them verse by verse, and recited them verbatim to his followers. These recitations circulated in the community as oral scriptures until they were later codified and published as one book, the Quran. The first written version of the Quran became available only two decades after the death of Muhammad.[5]

Like most prophets who came before him, Muhammad was ridiculed and treated with hostility in his hometown. He was eventually forced to flee to Medina, a city approximately two hundred miles north of Mecca. But in less than ten years he managed to recruit an army of volunteers in this city and march back to Mecca. After a fierce battle in 630 CE, Muhammad captured Mecca and announced the official founding of Islam.

The root word for Islam (*slm*) in Arabic denotes "submission." A Muslim is someone who has submitted his or her life to the will of Allah. A person can embrace Islam by saying a prayer of confession called *shahada*:

> *lā ilāha illà l-Lāh, Muhammadur rasūlu l-Lāh.*

> There is no god but Allah,
> Muhammad is the messenger of Allah.

True Muslims follow a common creed, which is often known as the "five pillars" of Islam. They recite the confession of faith (*shahada*); pray five times a day (*salat*); faithfully give a percentage of their earnings to the poor (*zakat*); fast during the month of Ramadan (*sawm*); and aspire to make the ultimate pilgrimage to Mecca (*hajj*), something that each Muslim is recommended to do at least once in a lifetime.

Two years after founding this new religion, Muhammad died unexpectedly without having named an official successor. A power struggle ensued, out of which two factions emerged: the group that supported Abu Bakr, the father-in-law of the prophet, came to be known as the Sunnis; and the group that followed Ali, the son-in-law of the prophet, the Shiites.[6] The rivalry between the factions grew steadily, but when Ali's son Husayn was killed in the Battle of Karbala in 661 CE, the division became irreconcilable. Even though both Sunni and Shia Muslims follow similar doctrines, they keep their distinct Islamic identities.

***

Dudley Woodberry is a professor of Islamic studies at Fuller Theological Seminary in Pasadena, California. Woodberry lived most of his life in Pakistan, soaking in the Islamic culture, and he is highly esteemed in secular as well as theological academia.

"Christians make an inadvertent mistake while they compare the Quran and the Bible," Woodberry tells the students in his class each semester. "A more appropriate comparison would be between the Quran and Jesus."

Students often scratch their heads, trying to make sense of this unlikely connection between a person and a book. But Woodberry's logic is quite simple.

Christians believe that "the Word," an eternal expression of God's mind, took flesh in the person of Jesus Christ. "In the beginning was the Word, the Word was with God and the Word was God," wrote the disciple John, as we have already seen in the previous chapter. "The Word became flesh and dwelt among us."[7] In Islam, the Word did not become a person, it rather appeared as a book. The Quran is the miracle creation (*I'jaz Al Quran*) that descended directly from heaven to reveal to us the mind of God.

In Woodberry's language, Jesus Christ is the Word incarnate; the Quran is the Word *"inlibriate."*

The marked-up and mutilated Gideon's Bible tucked under my pillow was just as authoritative for me as the Quran was for my friend Abdul. But while Christians consider the Bible to be the "inspired" word of God, Muslims consider the Quran a "literal" revelation from God.

The Quran is not written by a human author; rather it is a divine revelation that originated from a master book in heaven. Unlike many other sacred texts, it is considered the replica of an eternal "mother book" (*umm-ul-kitab*) that exists in a spiritual realm.[8]

The Bible is also a product of direct revelation from God, but it is expressed through the creative minds of a number of different authors, and historically conditioned within the context of a community. The power of the Bible, to a

Christian, lies in its ability to connect us to the "living Word," who is Jesus Christ.

Intriguingly, the Quran is the only non-Christian scripture that explicitly talks about the person of Jesus Christ. It refers to him as Isa, the prophet. There are many prophets in the Quran who are also mentioned in the Bible (Adam, Noah, Abraham, Moses, and so on). Jesus is one of those prophets who also received a special revelation (the Injil) from Allah.

As a matter of fact, the Quran paints an illustrious picture of Jesus, far more uniquely than any of the other prophets appearing in its pages.[9] Jesus' mother, Mary, is the only woman to be mentioned by name in the Quran. In fact, an entire chapter, Sura 19, is named after her. Jesus is mentioned fifty-nine times in ninety-two verses, as opposed to Muhammad, who is mentioned only four times (by name) in the Quran.

The Bible does not tell us a lot about Jesus' childhood, except a brief visit to the temple at the age of twelve. But the Quran provides a vivid picture of his infancy, with details that sound outlandish even to Christians. There are stories about the boy Jesus making living birds out of clay and the baby Jesus speaking while he was still in the cradle:[10]

> They said, "How can we speak to one who is in the cradle a child?" [Jesus] said, "Indeed, I am the servant of Allah. He has given me the Scripture and made me a prophet. And He has made me blessed wherever I am and has enjoined upon me prayer and zakath as long as I remain alive. And [made me] dutiful to my mother, and He has not made me a wretched tyrant. And peace is on me the day I was

born and the day I will die and the day I am raised alive."[11]

The Quran ascribes to Jesus specific titles that imply uniqueness, and even divinity to an extent. For example, it addresses Jesus as the "Word of God" (*Kalimattullah*)—a title that may mean nothing to Muslims, but to Christians, it is loaded with theological connotations. As noted before, in the Bible, "the Word" (logos) does not merely refer to words spoken from the mouth of a prophet or written on the parchment of a sacred text. Logos is a person, an incarnate expression of God's mind. For a Christian, the "Word of God" is a categorical assertion of Jesus' deity, and proof of his oneness with God.[12]

Does the Quran describe Jesus as the Word of God simply because Allah gave him the Injil? Perhaps! But why then is Moses, who received the Torah from Allah, called *Kalimullah* (the one who talked to God) and Muhammad, who received the Quran from Allah, called *Rasulullah* (the messenger of God)? The titles of all other prophets in Islam are characteristically different from the title *Kalimatin minhu*— which literally means word (*kalima*) from (*min*) him (*hu*), a title that the Quran uses exclusively to address Jesus.[13]

As I continued to read the Quran, I was surprised to note that it also describes Jesus as the Messiah (the Christ).[14]

"All prophets are messiahs," argued my friend Abdul. "It only means that Jesus was anointed by Allah as a prophet. All prophets are anointed by God and all of them can be considered messiahs."

But as I explored further, I found it wasn't that simple. Jesus is called the Messiah (*Al-Masih*), not "a" messiah. The

Quran ascribes the title Al Masih only to Jesus, just as the Bible attributes the title *Ho Christos* (the Christ) only to one person.

The title "the Messiah" does not come from a cultural vacuum. It is a term that has theological implications in Judaism and Christianity. The Messiah, in both Jewish and Christian traditions, is more than a prophet, a priest, or a king. He is a cosmic hero who will one day intervene in human history as the ultimate savior. He is the apocalyptic figure in Islam who is going to execute divine judgment on the day of the final reckoning and establish divine justice in the new world.

The Messiah is a title reserved for one person and one person alone. All prophets, in both the Bible and the Quran, are anointed for specific missions, but there is only one who is "the" Anointed—the One whom the world has been waiting for.

The amazing parallels between the Jesus of Christianity and the Jesus of Islam do not end there. I was surprised to note that Muslims, like Jews and Christians, believe in a "messianic age," where God is going to destroy the wicked and establish the righteous.[15] In Islam, believe it or not, Jesus is the prophet who is going to spearhead this apocalyptic campaign of Allah.[16] He is considered the climactic figure of human history, who will come back to establish a world in which everybody follows Islam, a life surrendered to God.

Listen to how one of the Hadiths, another authoritative scripture of Islam, describes the second coming of Jesus:

> He will descend (to the earth) . . .
> He will fight for the cause of Islam . . .

He will break the cross, kill the swine,
and put an end to war . . .
He will destroy the Antichrist.[17]

Why is Jesus the only prophet who gets the title "the Messiah"? Why is he the only one who gets to come back to the world? It looks like there is more to him than meets the eye.

***

Abdul did not celebrate Christmas. But he believed in the story of Christmas, much more than many Christians who actually celebrated it.

The birth of Jesus, according to the Quran, is a "one-of-a-kind" miracle. First of all, the story affirms the "immaculate conception" of Jesus, which means that he was born of a virgin, kept purified specifically for this very purpose. Also, the Quranic narrative of Jesus' birth is strikingly similar to that of the Bible, with some added details.

In the Quranic version of the event, an exhausted Mary chances upon a stream that appears miraculously in the desert. She drinks the water from the stream, and gives birth to Jesus under a palm tree.

> So she conceived him, and she withdrew with him to a remote place. And the pains of childbirth drove her to the trunk of a palm tree. She said, "Oh, I wish I had died before this and was in oblivion, forgotten." But he called her from below her, "Do not grieve; your Lord has provided beneath you a stream. And shake toward you the trunk of the palm tree; it will drop upon you ripe, fresh dates. So eat and drink and be contented. And if you see from among humanity anyone, say, 'Indeed, I have

> vowed to the Most Merciful abstention, so I will
> not speak today to [any] man." Then she
> brought him to her people, carrying him.[18]

I have come across many Christians who find the miracle of the virgin birth far too difficult to believe. While conservative Christians generally hold the gospel story to be infallible, those in the "progressive" camp view certain elements of it to be allegorical or mythological. The virgin birth is one such area of disagreement. But Islam does not allow scientific rationalism to displace this miracle; it embraces the historicity of Jesus' virgin birth without a question.

How can a Muslim believe Jesus was born without a human father, and yet deny the fact that he was more than a mere mortal? I asked Abdul.

Apparently I was not the first to pose this question. A group of Christians in Narjan, a city in the southern states of Arabia, once approached Muhammad and raised the same question. At first the prophet seemed to have no answer. But later, the angel gave him the following revelation:[19]

> Indeed, the example of Jesus to Allah is like that
> of Adam. He created Him from dust; then He
> said to him, 'Be,' and he was.[20]

Jesus is not the only human being born without a father. God created Adam also without a human progenitor. The virgin birth of Jesus, Muhammad therefore argued, is not a unique miracle with any theological significance.[21]

In my opinion, however, the difference between the creation of Adam and the birth of Jesus is too substantial to compare. For starters, Adam was never born. He was created "as is"—a fully formed adult male, not born of a father or mother.[22] As the first human being, this was the only logical way that he could have been brought into existence. The "birth" of Adam, therefore, was by no means extraordinary; it was the only plausible option for the creation of the first human on earth.

Jesus, on the other hand, could have been brought into the world in a number of different ways. He could have been created from dust like Adam, or born naturally like all the other prophets. Yet we read in the Quran that he was birthed by the Holy Spirit, which means the Spirit had to enter a human womb and initiate the natural course of pregnancy and childbirth.[23]

This is why the Quran calls Jesus a "Spirit from God."[24] The life of all creatures originates from God. In that sense, we are all spirits from God. But Jesus was the only human being to be conceived without an earthly father. He was, in a literal sense, conceived of the Spirit of God.

The presence of the Spirit was not confined to Jesus' conception alone; the Holy Spirit controlled his life and ministry as well.[25] The Quran summarizes his eventful life into a single verse: "And I (Jesus) heal those born blind, and the lepers, and I quicken the dead."[26] The Holy Spirit animated Jesus' life, formed his identity, and anointed his ministry.

The question now looms large. What was so special about Jesus that prompted God to alter the natural order of procreation and "beget" him in a virgin's womb? According to both the Quran and the Bible, this was the only time in human history something like this has ever happened. Why didn't God use this specific birthing process for Abraham,

Moses, or Muhammad? What was so unique about Jesus that his arrival on the earth had to be engineered in such a special way?

"What if we did a paternity test on Jesus?" I asked Abdul again. "What would we find?"

Jesus's DNA should find a match in Mary as his mother, but what would it reveal about his father?

"Who do you think the father of Jesus is?" I rephrased the question.

I pictured in my mind a talk show host ripping open an envelope and screaming at God, "You are the father!" If Jesus was conceived of the Spirit of God without a human father, as the Quran claims him to be, the paternity test should show, so to speak, God's DNA.

Abdul hesitated for a moment at my question, and responded with caution.

"It has to be God. He created Jesus with His Spirit."

"If God is Jesus' father, why are you offended when I call him the Son of God?" I asked.

This is where Abdul drew the line. An anthropomorphic representation of God—portraying God with human attributes—is a grievous blasphemy in Islamic tradition. The Quran objects to it in harsh language:

> And they say, "The Most Merciful has taken [for Himself] a son." You have done an atrocious thing. The heavens almost rupture therefrom and the earth splits open and the mountains collapse in devastation. That they attribute to the Most Merciful a son. And it is not

appropriate for the Most Merciful that He should take a son."[27]

The Quran's logic is simple and straightforward: God cannot beget a child without a consort.[28] If Jesus is depicted as the Son of God, it implies that God had sex with Mary to conceive him.

I tried to explain to Abdul the idea of a theological metaphor. The title "Son of God" is a symbolic term that the Bible uses to describe the divine nature Jesus shares with God.[29] When we describe someone as a "son of a gun," it represents a defining characteristic of the person—that the nature of the man is like that of a gun: volatile, dangerous, and unpredictable—not, of course, that the gun has some kind of claim to his paternity. When I look at a baby and make a comment such as "she is her father's daughter" or "he is his mother's son," I am actually referring to the unique characteristics the child shares with its father or mother.

In the same way, when Christians describe Jesus as the Son of God, they are not talking about God having sex with a mortal woman to produce a human child. What they actually mean is that Jesus exhibits the very attributes only God possesses, and in that sense, he is the most tangible expression of God we have ever seen in this world. In other words, Jesus is the exact representation of God, whom he called his Father.

It is the irony. Islam vehemently denies any proposition that suggests Jesus was more than a man, but the depiction of his virgin birth in the Quran undoubtedly points to the fact that he was more than mere human. A child conceived without human sperm, by mere logic, should be "super-human," to say the least.

Abdul was not convinced, but the plot thickens as the Jesus story unfolds in the pages of the Quran. The mysterious beginning of this man is bookended with an even more mysterious ending.

***

Under the snow-covered mountains of Srinagar, a city in the northern part of India, there is a tomb that attracts thousands of visitors every season. A sect of Islam, known as "Ahammadiya," claims this to be the tomb of Jesus. In their interpretation of the story of Jesus' crucifixion, he only lost consciousness on the cross. Jesus was buried before his actual death, and later revived in the tomb. He then traveled east, all the way to India, where he died an old man.

Orthodox Muslims dispel this story as a fanciful hoax. Even the very thought of Jesus's death is an outright blasphemy to a Muslim. The Quran rebukes, and even taunts, Jesus' captors for claiming that they killed him:

> And [for] their saying, "Indeed, we have killed the Messiah, Jesus, the son of Mary, the messenger of Allah." And they did not kill him, nor did they crucify him; but [another] was made to resemble him to them . . . And they did not kill him, for certain.[30]

In the Islamic version of the crucifixion, "the Jews" think that they nailed Jesus to the cross, but the joke was on them. It was not Jesus, but a substitute that died in his place. What happened on the cross was nothing but an illusion. God played a trick, mass hypnotism of sorts, making the body on the cross resemble (*shubbiha lahum*) that of Jesus.[31]

In one of the many legends circulating in the Islamic world, God made all his disciples look like Jesus at the time of crucifixion. In the end, one of them, most probably Judas Iscariot, ended up getting crucified. In another story, Simon of Cyrene volunteered to die on behalf of Jesus. In yet other stories, the Jewish leaders intentionally killed someone else (most probably one of the guards who arrested him), because the real Jesus slipped through their hands.[32]

In all these versions, Jesus does not die on the cross. Instead Allah takes him directly to Himself. "O Jesus, indeed I will take you and raise you to Myself," says Allah. "And purify you from those who disbelieve and make those who follow you [in submission to Allah alone] superior to those who disbelieve until the Day of Resurrection."[33] Jesus now lives in paradise, counting the days of his return to the world as the apocalyptic Messiah.

The death of Jesus, however, is an undeniable historical event. Scholars have successfully retold the story of his life and death using historical records and archeological evidence. An exploration of the quest for historical Jesus is beyond the scope of this chapter, but let me draw your attention to two non-Christian sources, one Jewish and the other Roman.

Flavius Josephus, one of the most noted first-century Jewish historians, writes about Jesus's death in his celebrated book, *Antiquities of the Jews* (93-94 CE):

> When Pilate, upon hearing him accused by the men of the highest standing among us, had condemned him to be crucified . . .[34]

The esteemed Roman historian Tacitus, who wrote elaborately about first-century Rome, describes Jesus' execution by Pontius Pilate in his *Annals of Imperial Rome* (117 CE):

> Christus, the founder of the name, had undergone death penalty in the reign of Tiberius, by sentence of the procurator Pontius Pilate.[35]

The evidence clearly establishes Jesus' crucifixion as a historical reality. The Roman soldiers were well trained to verify the identity of a culprit before they crucified him, and to confirm his death before they buried the corpse. It is very unlikely that the authorities could have been fooled by an illusion or mass hypnotism.

We have also seen that the Quran confirms a Jewish plot that existed against Jesus. Therefore some Islamic scholars believe that the Quran, at the very least, alludes to Jesus' death on the cross.[36] For example, let us refer back to Jesus' cradle speech:

"Peace is on me the day I was born and the day I will die and the day I am raised alive."[37]

In this verse Jesus seems to be predicting his own death. In another verse, his death is considered a statistical probability based solely on the history of Israel's treatment of other prophets:

> We gave Moses the Book and followed him up with a succession of apostles; We gave Jesus the son of Mary clear [signs] and strengthened him with the holy spirit. Is it that whenever there comes to you an apostle with what ye yourselves desire not, ye are puffed up with pride? Some ye called impostors, and others ye slay![38]

Why, then, would Islam vehemently deny the death of Jesus?

"Allah cannot let an innocent man suffer such injustice. That's why," answered Abdul.

But it is not the first time an innocent man is falsely accused and murdered by the enemies of God, even within the pages of the Quran. Countless prophets have been persecuted and martyred while they were on their God-given missions. Why should Allah be so protective of Jesus?

"He was not like any other prophets," clarified Abdul. "He was not just innocent. He was also pure and holy."

Jesus was more than a prophet. The prophets reminded people of their sins and called them to repentance. But at the same time, they were not immune to the problem of sin. In the Quran even Muhammad was charged with sins against Allah on many occasions.[39] But Jesus, unlike all other prophets, was destined for a holy life right from his mother's womb. The angel testified that the child Mary was going to carry would be a "faultless boy."[40] The Hadiths report, "no child is born but he is pricked by the Satan and he begins to weep because of the pricking of the Satan except the son of Mary and his mother."[41]

Both Christians and Muslims believe that Jesus led a sinless life. In fact he is the only one to have done so. This is why the Quran considers the life and ministry of Jesus so unique that it is "distinguished in this world and the Hereafter and among those brought near [to Allah]."[42]

There has never been a perfect man to live in this world, except for Jesus. He cannot be consumed by death like everyone else.

***

One of the most festive celebrations I remember from my childhood days was *Bakrid*, the Islamic festival also known as *Eid al-Adha* in most parts of the world. It was also a school holiday, so we would walk around the town greeting people "*Id Mubarak*," and receiving gifts, which usually came in the form of candies. Muslim families also invited us to be part of a great feast that they served on that day.

The Eid feast is prepared from the meat of a goat or a sheep, ritually sacrificed (*qurban*) to Allah. The animal symbolizes a lamb, which Abraham sacrificed to God in the place of his son.

In the Bible, God asks Abraham to offer his son Isaac as a sacrifice.[43] But in the Quran's version of the story, it is not Isaac but Ishmael who ends up on the altar.[44]

In order to understand the significance of Eid al-Adha, we must first consider the meaning of religious sacrifice in general. In the other Abrahamic religions, sacrifice serves as a symbol of substitutionary death, where the blood of the animal takes away the sins of the penitent offeror. But the concept of sin in Islam is a bit different. Muslims do not believe in the inherent sinful nature of humanity. Sin is a rebellion against the commandments of Allah. Salvation is, therefore, a matter of obedience and submission to Allah's commandments. There is no necessity for "atonement" of any kind.

Why, then, is the ritual of sacrifice so important in Islam? In another episode in the Quran, God asks Moses to sacrifice an unblemished cow, neither too young nor too old, and yellow in color.[45] This sacrificial animal even has the power to resurrect those who are dead: "So We said: Strike the [dead body] with part of the [sacrificed cow], Allah brings the dead to life, and He shows you His signs so that you may understand."[46]Although Muslims do not attribute a deeper meaning to the ritual of sacrifice the way the Christians or the Jews do, the Quran seems to suggest otherwise.

The passage describing Eid al-Adha is very conclusive in suggesting that Allah "ransomed" Ishmael with a great sacrifice.[47] But what was the ransom that was paid off through this great sacrifice? If Allah could redeem people at His will, why was a ransom necessary for Ishmael? This question takes us to another irony in Islam: "We have in Islam the great anomaly of a religion which rejects the doctrine of sacrifice for sin, whilst its great central feast is a feast of sacrifice."[48]

In Christianity, the animal ransomed for Abraham's son foreshadows the Lamb of God that is ransomed for us— Jesus. But in Islam, the death of Jesus is not required; no ransom is needed.

Now we see why Islam protests the death of Jesus: if Jesus of the Quran died, Islam has to reconcile the fact that God did not vindicate this faultless prophet. Jesus is not just another innocent victim; he is pure and sinless. He therefore could not have been martyred just like any other prophet. God cannot desert or disown the only sinless person ever to have lived on this planet. If Allah let him die on the cross, He would become a co-conspirator in the most heinous crime committed in human history. This is a serious moral problem in the eyes of Islam.

Christianity suggests that the only way to make sense of this paradox is to attribute a redemptive meaning to Jesus' death. Is it possible that Jesus was our ransom in a cosmic Eid al-Adha, his blood truly the atonement for our sins, and his cross the altar of sacrifice in which God prevented the ultimate human tragedy? One needs to go to the Jesus of the Bible to find the answers.

***

One quiet Monday morning my telephone rang unexpectedly. The person on the other end introduced herself as Fatima, a PhD candidate at one of the most prestigious universities in North America.

Her question startled me: "Can I talk to someone about Jesus?"

Fatima was a devout Muslim immigrant from a Pakistani family, and she had a bizarre story to tell.

Fatima had visited an art gallery in Montreal a week before. As she was browsing the paintings she chanced upon one in particular—an angry mob getting ready to stone a distraught woman. The woman is begging for mercy. Between the woman and the mob is a man hunched over on the ground. He is scribbling something on the sand with his fingers.

The title read: "Casting the First Stone."

I have seen different renditions of this gospel episode on canvas. But none of them have ever moved me to the extent that Fatima was describing.

"I started crying," said Fatima. "I don't know why. I just wanted to see his face."

Jesus was no stranger to Fatima. She had known him as one of the many prophets in the Quran. But this was nothing less than a transcendent encounter.

Fatima and I eventually became good friends. We had many interesting conversations about Islam and Christianity, but her favorite topic of all was Jesus.

"I did not understand the power of forgiveness before I met Jesus," Fatima said to me one day. In the Quran, Allah forgives at His will. But it comes with many strings attached. In the end, one is not really sure whether she is forgiven or not. "That has never made sense to me. It feels unreal. I needed to hear a voice like that woman in the painting did."

Fatima found true forgiveness in the sacrifice of Jesus. Today she considers herself a Christ-follower who happens to be a Muslim.

My college roommate Abdul took a different route. For him, religion is more about observing God's law than entering into a relationship with Him. Unlike the God of the Bible, Allah does not express any desire for a "personal relationship" with His devotees. He is a sovereign judge who demands from us only one thing—strict obedience to His commandments.

Abdul had been a practicing Muslim all his life. Yet he cringed every time I prayed, "Our Father in heaven." He never thought he could be considered a child of God, and he never dared to call God "Father." The best Abdul could ever be was His servant; in fact, the name Abdul itself is a prefix that means a "servant of."

In the end, Islam and Christianity may intersect in complex and inextricable ways, but they are far from being identical. One calls us into obedience to a book, and the other into relationship with a person.

Abdul found the best expression of God's mind in the Quran. Fatima found it in Jesus Christ.

The Wise Men of the East foresaw this person, entering the world through the womb of a virgin. Perhaps they knew that he would one day become a "sign unto all men" by hanging on the altar of Eid al-Adah. By offering his own life as "qurban," he would reconcile the broken relationship between God and humanity. But that would not be the end. As both Islam and Christianity anticipate, he is going to come back again to establish a new Kingdom—the domain of God in which everyone leads a life surrendered to His will.

We are waiting for the return of the King.

THE PIERCED MESSIAH

"Then they will look on me whom they have pierced... Yes, they will mourn for Him as one mourns for his only son."

Zechariah 12:10

It is very unlikely that someone in India would grow up in an environment steeped in Jewish culture. I had that privilege. I went to college in Kochi, a city that was home to one of the country's early Jewish settlements. The Jewish diaspora in Kochi claims its heritage all the way back to the arrival of Israeli traders from the kingdom of Solomon.

"Jew Street" in Kochi is still the hub of business and commerce. One of the major tourist attractions in the city is a synagogue, currently preserved as a national heritage site by the local government. It showcases an amazing display of cultural artifacts: ceramic tiles from China, hand embroidered rugs from Ethiopia, candelabras from Belgium and so on.

I used to frequent the Jewish town during my lunch hour in college. I remember buying challah bread from a store painted in the colors of the Israeli flag. It had a seven-branched *menorah*, the Jewish lamp, showcased on the shop window. A Star of David was engraved on its door and a *mezuzah*, a parchment scroll that contains verses from the *Torah*, the Jewish Scripture, tucked inside the lintels.

As a student, I was fascinated by the history of the Jewish people. I knew that many legendary figures who had changed the course of human history were Jewish—Baruch Spinoza, Sigmund Freud, Albert Einstein, Karl Marx, Steven Spielberg . . . and of course, Jesus of Nazareth.

Theoretically speaking, anyone can accept Judaism through a binding ritual of consent, which affirms faith in the covenants God established through Abraham, Moses, and David.[1] But the Jews generally believe that people inherit their religion. A person born to Jewish parents is considered a Jew even if he or she does not practice the religion. A non-Jew who believes and observes the Jewish laws, on the other hand, may still be considered a Gentile.

Judaism is classified primarily into three categories based on its theological conventions: "Orthodox Judaism" attempts to practice strict observances of the Jewish law and cultural traditions, paying high regard to the rabbinic interpretations of the *mitzvoth*, the specific commandments of the law.[2] "Reform Judaism" strives to adapt to the religious practices and objectives of modern society by concentrating more on the ethical aspects of religion than on traditional laws and Scriptures. "Conservative Judaism" aims to preserve those religious practices that are deemed meaningful, while eliminating those that are considered irrelevant in the modern day.

Judaism may be the smallest of all the major religions in the world, but it is the parent religion of two of the largest ones: Christianity and Islam. As a matter of fact, Judaism is much more than a religion. It has inherent connections to race, culture, and national identity. I have often heard people making statements such as, "I am Jewish, but not religious." I have also met Jews who confess Jesus as their Messiah and worship him as God. They describe themselves as "Messianic Jews," not (merely) as Christians.

In college, I had a friend named Solomon. No one knew he was Jewish until he started talking about his family's plan to migrate to Israel. Solomon looked like an Indian, spoke fluent Hindi, and waxed eloquently on Bollywood films. So it came as a big surprise to all of us to find out that he truly belonged somewhere else. Solomon had always dreamed of going to the Promised Land.

The idea of a Promised Land is central to Judaism. The Jewish people believe that the land of Israel is their covenantal right from God. It is considered a mitzvah to live in Israel. The Jewish people all over the world, including Kochi, conclude their holiday celebrations with a benediction: "Next Year in Jerusalem!"

India once had a thriving Jewish community. At its peak, it claimed to have at least seven synagogues and over two thousand Jews. Today only a handful of them remain in the country. Most have immigrated to the Promised Land, like my friend Solomon.

Solomon left for Israel soon after his graduation. I have not heard from him since.

Today, as an Indian living in the US, I am also part of a diasporic culture. But I have never felt the same nostalgia

Solomon felt for "home." Unlike me, he had been longing for a home that he had never seen.

My home is where my heart is. But Solomon's heart was where his home was.

***

In 2005, Mel Gibson's *The Passion of the Christ* took Hollywood by storm. The film recreated Jesus' last days on the earth, leading up to his crucifixion. Gibson took painstaking efforts to stay faithful to the gospel texts, and even shot the film in Aramaic, the language widely used in first-century Palestine. It was indeed a passion project for the actor-turned-director.

Despite mixed reviews from the audience, the film turned out to be a blockbuster hit at the box office. Critics, however, disparaged the film, accusing it of "Jewish stereotyping" and of having historical inaccuracies. The media portrayed Gibson as a bigot and an anti-Semite, as the film attributed much of the blame for Jesus' crucifixion to the Jewish people.

I struggled to understand what the fuss was all about. Gibson was only following the gospel narrative, I thought, which clearly points to a Jewish plot to murder Jesus.[3] I couldn't help but look at him as the victim of a witch-hunt by the liberal media. But soon after watching *The Passion of the Christ*, I wrote a paper for a university course on Film and Religion, which prodded me to see some of these accusations in a different light.

My essay was on a particular theological issue the scholars call "deicide controversy." The term "deicide" literally means "murder of God." The Jews are often accused of deicide because the gospels attribute the primary responsibility for Jesus' crucifixion to them.

As the Roman Empire became Christian, the deicide propaganda turned deadly, and people began to describe the Jews as "Christ-killers." It did not take long for Christian anti-Judaism to turn into genocidal anti-Semitism. The Fourth Lateran Council of 1215, for example, insisted that Jews had to distinguish themselves from Christians with a different dress code. They were banned from appearing in public on special Christian festivals. Even the Jewish converts to Christianity were labeled *"marranos"* (pigs) in medieval Europe, and were targeted in the Spanish Inquisition.

Christians also launched many false accusations against the Jews, including witchcraft, ritual murder, and even poisoning wells. The notorious "blood libel," an accusation that the Jews used human blood in making their ceremonial bread, began in the Middle Ages and continued until the early twentieth century. The hatred against the "Christ-killers" eventually metastasized into widespread anti-Semitism, and culminated in the Holocaust. As Nicholas Berdyaev puts it, "those who rejected the cross had to carry it, while those who welcomed it were often engaged in crucifying others."[4]

Today Christians have come to realize the tragic consequences of the deicide controversy. *Nostra Aetate* (In our Age: Declaration of the Relationship of the Church to Non-Christian Religions), a document issued by the Catholic Church, affirms that the Jewish covenantal bond with God still remains valid despite the arrival of Christianity. "True, the Jewish authorities and those who followed their lead pressed for the death of Christ," says the Church. "Still, what happened in His passion cannot be charged against all the Jews, without distinction, then alive, nor against the Jews of today. Although the Church is the new people of God, the Jews should not be presented as rejected or accursed by God, as if this followed from the Holy Scriptures."[5] The Church also affirms that the cross of Christ has reconciled both the Jews and the Gentiles to God, making them part of one family.

There is an increased interest in Christian–Jewish dialogues in the Protestant circles as well. Jürgen Moltmann, an esteemed Protestant theologian, describes Christianity an extension of the Jewish mission to the world, in anticipation of the "*eschaton*"—the end of this earth—awaited by both.[6] Christianity does not supersede Judaism; it rather universalizes the Jewish religion. The salvation of Israel will come when the full measure of Gentiles is brought into Christ.

Jewish scholars, by the same token, also appreciate the fact that Christians worship the Jewish God, and that they accept the moral principles of the Torah. They affirm that the "relationship between Jews and Christians will not weaken Jewish practice."[7] Some rabbis even suggest that it might be appropriate for the Gentiles to believe in God's manifestation in Christ, even though such a belief is prohibited for the Jews.

A group of prominent Orthodox rabbis recently issued a statement titled, *To Do the Will of Our Father in Heaven: Toward a Partnership between Jews and Christians*,[8] in which Christianity is described as "the willed divine outcome and gift to the nations." "Jesus brought a double goodness to the world," say the rabbis. "On the one hand he strengthened the Torah of Moses majestically" and on the other hand, "he removed idols from the nations," instilling them "firmly with moral traits." They applaud Christians for their work for the sake of the Kingdom of God, and promise that their "reward will not be denied."

We can now confidently say that after a long history of hatred and violence, the deicide controversy has finally died down. After all, if we believe Jesus died for our sins, then it is "we," not just the Jews nor the Romans, who crucified Him. Each of us bears the responsibility for Jesus' death on the cross.

There is good news, however. Jesus forgave those who crucified him at the cross itself. He proclaimed repeatedly during his ministry that the purpose of his coming to the world was "to give His life a ransom for many."[9] One of the posters of *The Passion of the Christ* reminds us of this truth in a profound way:

"Dying was the reason for His living."

***

Jesus was a Jew. He was raised under the Jewish law, reading the Jewish Scriptures. He attended the Jewish synagogue[10] and faithfully celebrated the Jewish feasts.[11] As Eugene Fisher puts it, "the denial of Jesus' Jewishness is the denial of his humanity."[12]

Many Jewish historians picture Jesus as a political revolutionary of his time. Some consider him an Essene monk in the light of the Dead Sea scrolls, and others an eschatological prophet in the tradition of their apocalyptical literature. But who is Jesus to a Jew today?

Most Jews think of Jesus as a charismatic rabbi who lived in first-century Palestine. The gospels frequently address him by this title. There were two Pharisaic schools present at the time, one run by Rabbi Shammai and the other by Rabbi Hillel. The teachings of Jesus resembled closely to those of Hillel, and for this reason, some scholars think Jesus was a rabbi trained at the school of Hillel.

The pattern of Jesus' life fit the life of a rabbi of his time. His teachings were firmly grounded in the Jewish law. He clearly stated that he came "not to destroy the Law, but to fulfill it."[13] Unlike other rabbis, however, he gave new meaning and interpretation to the Law, which became scandalous and blasphemous to many ears. Moreover, he invited Gentiles into a relationship with the Jewish God, which called into question Israel's privileged status as the chosen people of God.

How did an ordinary rabbi become one of the most influential figures in human history? Especially one who was born and raised in a working class family, lived only thirty-odd years, never went to a formal school, never wrote a book, was neither a soldier nor a political leader?

Is it possible that Jesus was more than a rabbi or a prophet? First-century Jewish historian Flavius Josephus, while introducing Jesus in his book *Antiquities of the Jews*, wondered, "About this time there lived Jesus, a wise man, if indeed one ought to call him a man."[14] It looks like the contemporaries of Jesus thought of him as more than mere human. Some Jews even believed he was God in human flesh, and they later came to be known as "Christians."

Of course, it is sacrilegious for Jews to conceive God in human form. "[God] has no semblance of a body nor is He corporeal," says a Jewish prayer.[15] The third of *The Thirteen Principles of Faith* by Moses Maimonides, an early Jewish rabbi, emphatically declares that "the Creator, Blessed is His Name, is not physical and is not affected by physical phenomena, and that there is no comparison whatsoever to Him."[16] In the Jewish worldview, divinity and humanity are mutually exclusive and irreconcilable.

The Jewish Scriptures, however, seem to think otherwise. In the Genesis account of creation, God creates humanity in His "image and likeness." If that is the case, perfect humanity, hypothetically speaking, is a mirror reflection of perfect divinity. The image of God and the image of man, though not the same, need not be mutually exclusive. As paradoxical as it sounds, according to Jewish theology, it is completely logical to believe that a perfect God can express Himself as a perfect man.

We see many accounts in the Scriptures where God presents Himself in human form. When "the Lord appears" to Abraham, for example, what we actually see is three men entering his house, washing their feet, and eating a meal.[17] In another episode, a mysterious person wrestles with Jacob and dislocates his thigh. We don't know who this man is, but Jacob recollects, "I have seen God face to face."[18] A few centuries later, a stranger approaches Joshua with a drawn sword in his hands. Joshua immediately removes sandals from his feet and "falls on his face to the earth and bows down" as an act of worship.[19] In the book of Daniel, three Jewish boys are thrown into a blazing furnace. Suddenly a fourth person who looks like "a son of the gods" appears in the middle of the fire.[20]

Theologians describe these events as "theophanies"—human encounters with the divine. Christians consider these theophanies to be "Christophanies," or the preincarnate appearances of Christ.

The prophets of Israel witnessed God experiencing, and even expressing, human emotions such as anger, love, grief, passion, and even hatred.[21] They also recorded a series of esoteric visions in which He would one day enter the world in human form. Isaiah, for example, saw God visiting the earth as a child born of a virgin. It would be the beginning of a new era in which the transcendent God becomes immanent and is called "Immanuel"—God who is with us.[22]

***

The Jews are a people in waiting. Over the last four millennia of their recorded history, they have been subjugated by a number of political superpowers: Egyptians, Babylonians, Persians, Greeks, Romans . . . the list goes on. Even after becoming an independent nation state a few decades ago, Israel has no lack of enemies.

Throughout these periodic episodes of oppression, the Jews have been waiting faithfully for a promised savior. God has promised them a deliverer, an eternal king who is going to establish an everlasting kingdom. This promise was an integral part of God's covenant with David:

> I will raise up your descendant after you, who will come forth from you, and I will establish his kingdom. He shall build a house for My name, and I will establish the throne of his kingdom forever. . . . Your house and your kingdom shall endure before Me forever; your throne shall be established forever.[23]

The title of this future leader of Israel is "the Messiah." The word Messiah comes from the verb *m-sh-h* (to anoint), which represents the anointing ritual for a priest or a king. In that sense, all anointed officials are messiahs. The

112

Scriptures address even Cyrus, a Persian king who helped with the restoration of Israel from Babylonian captivity, a messiah.[24]

"The Messiah," however, is different from a messiah. According to the Jewish faith, the Messiah is "a charismatically endowed descendant of David . . . raised up by God to break the yoke of the heathen, to reign over the restored kingdom of Israel."[25] He is the iconic savior figure in Jewish "mythology" who will establish the righteous rule of God in this world.

The prophets envisioned the Messiah to be a mythical hero. "I will raise to David a Branch of righteousness," said Jeremiah. "A King shall reign and prosper, and execute judgment and righteousness in the earth. In His days Judah will be saved, and Israel will dwell safely; Now this is His name by which He will be called: The Lord our Righteousness."[26] Malachi predicted that Elijah would reappear and herald the coming of the Messiah.[27] Another prophet, Zechariah, described in vivid detail the bloody battle that would take place at the Messiah's arrival.[28]

The rabbinic traditions still believe that "the Messianic Redemption will be ushered in by a person, a human leader, a descendant of the kings David and Solomon, who will reinstate the Davidic royal dynasty."[29] The twelfth of *The Thirteen Principles of Faith* reminds the Jews that "though the Messiah delays, one must constantly expect His coming."[30]

In every generation there is an individual, "a scion of the House of David," who has "the potential to be the Messiah."[31] Maimonides postulates a set of criteria for identifying him: if we see a Jewish leader who (a) toils in the study of the Torah and is meticulous about the observance of the mitzvoth, (b) influences the Jews to follow the ways of the Torah, and (c) wages the "battles of G-d"—such a person is the "presumptive Messiah." Based on Maimonides' description, the Messiah will be both a ruler and a teacher.

The Jewish nation has also had its own share of pseudo-messiahs in its history. A man named Simon bar Kokhba, for example, declared himself to be the Messiah almost a century after Jesus' death when the Romans decided to build a city on the ruins of Jerusalem. He led a partially successful revolt (132–135 CE) against the empire and reclaimed the land of Palestine as a Jewish state. But the Romans soon thwarted the revolution and prohibited the Jews from even entering the city. Another self-proclaimed Messiah named Shabbatai Tzvi (1626–1676 CE) emerged during the Ottoman period, promising the restoration of Israel. Jews all over the world sold their possessions and headed toward the Promised Land. But the Sultan of Turkey arrested Tzvi and offered him a choice—death or conversion to Islam. Tzvi converted, and saved his life.

The history of Israel is riddled with such tragic stories of fallen messiahs. Failed messiahs brought disaster; traitorous messiahs caused disappointment. Today many Jews downplay the idea of a messianic redemption. Some speculate that the Messiah has already come at some point in history and will not be returning.[32] Others interpret the "shoah" (the Holocaust) and the emergence of the state of Israel as "birth pangs of the Messiah," who is about to come.[33]

As a Christian, I was taught to believe that Jesus was the Jewish Messiah. After all, the Hebrew Scriptures have already given us his résumé. We know the Messiah's gender (male), his family (Judah), and even the city in which he was to be born (Bethlehem).[34] Obviously Jesus fits the profile. Certain editions of the Bible have a comparison chart that shows how different events in Jesus' life fulfill the messianic prophecies of the Hebrew Scriptures. But my Jewish friends find such comparisons farfetched, and even downright offensive.

"The messianic prophecies are not fulfilled until and unless the Jewish nation triumphs over the world," says one of my rabbi friends from Toronto. The Messiah will reestablish the political sovereignty of Israel. He will rebuild the Holy Temple in Jerusalem. All exiles will return to the Promised Land, including the "ten lost tribes." There will be universal disarmament and worldwide peace, and the whole world will come to acknowledge and serve the Jewish God.[35] Obviously Jesus has failed to accomplish all of these important messianic tasks, at least while he was here on earth.

So, the Jews are still waiting for their Messiah.

***

Superman, the iconic action hero from the cartoon world, is known as the Man of Steel all over Metropolis. Only a few are aware of the fact that the clumsy reporter at the *Daily Planet*, Clark Kent, is his alter ego. We cannot pick between Clark Kent and Superman. They are one.

The Messiah is the Superman of the Jewish Scriptures. He is the transcendent hero who is going to fly in from outer space to save the world at the time of apocalypse. But on occasions, the same Scriptures also record cryptic visions of this superhero's alter ego. "And I will pour on the house of

David and on the inhabitants of Jerusalem the Spirit of grace and supplication; then they will look on me whom they have pierced," cries out Zechariah. "Yes, they will mourn for Him as one mourns for his only son, and grieve for Him as one grieves for a firstborn."[36]

A pierced Messiah? It is a dramatically different picture from the one the Jews have in mind. A suffering hero does not match the criteria they have set for the promised savior. But this alter ego keeps appearing sporadically in the visions of the prophets. Isaiah, for example, sees the picture of a bruised and battered Messiah, and describes it in vivid detail:[37]

> He has no stately form or majesty
> That we should look upon Him,
> Nor appearance that we should be attracted to Him.
> He was despised and forsaken of men,
> A man of sorrows and acquainted with grief;
> And like one from whom men hide their face
> He was despised, and we did not esteem Him.
> Surely our griefs He Himself bore,
> And our sorrows He carried;
> Yet we ourselves esteemed Him stricken,
> Smitten of God, and afflicted.
> But He was pierced through for our transgressions,
> He was crushed for our iniquities;
> The chastening for our well-being fell upon Him,
> And by His scourging we are healed.
> All of us like sheep have gone astray,
> Each of us has turned to his own way;
> But the Lord has caused the iniquity of us all
> To fall on Him.

The Jewish scholars struggle to reconcile these conflicting pictures of their savior—the triumphant superhero and his suffering alter ego. A number of them believe that there could be two distinct Messiahs instead of the one God had originally promised. "The dilemma was solved by splitting the person of the Messiah in two," says Raphael Patai, a Jewish scholar. "One of them, called Messiah ben Joseph, was to raise the armies of Israel against their enemies, and after many victories and miracles, would fall victim to Gog and Magog. The other, Messiah ben David, will come after him, and will lead Israel to the ultimate victory, the triumph, and the Messianic era of bliss."[38] According to this theory, Messiah ben David (son of David) is the superhero and Messiah ben Joseph (son of Joseph) is his alter ego.[39]

In certain Talmudic writings, Messiah ben Joseph is resurrected after his death in the battle between the kingdom of Gog and Magog:

> And when he will see that Messiah ben Joseph will be slain, he will say before Him: "Master of the World! I ask nothing of you except life!" God will say to him: "Even before you said, 'life,' your father David prophesied about you as it is written, He asked life of thee, Thou gavest it him." [40]

This "double identity" of the Messiah is a baffling concept for the Jewish scholars. But the New Testament Scriptures propose a solution—what if both these messianic figures converge in one person?

According to Christian theology, Jesus of Nazareth, the Jewish rabbi from first-century Palestine, is both a suffering servant and a sovereign king. "It did not take much time for me to realize that both these portrayals of the Messiah are pointing to one savior figure," says Sharon, a Messianic Jew I met in Los Angeles. "He will lead his people to the ultimate victory over evil in the future (as the son of David), while vicariously identifying with their pain, suffering, and even death (as the son of Joseph) at the present."

Jesus came to this world as the son of Joseph once, and will be coming back again as the son of David. The entire world, including the Jewish people, will look upon "the one whom they pierced," and realize that he was indeed the promised savior.[41]

The Messiah, for the time being, is hiding in plain sight.

***

I have never attended a Passover meal. The closest I have come to it so far is the Seder meal some churches put together during Easter week. But my Jewish friends consider this mock-Passover celebration a misguided attempt to mimic a religious ritual rightfully belonging only to them.

Passover (*Pesach*) commemorates an event in the history of Israel in which the angel of death "passed over" the Jewish homes, sparing the lives of their firstborn sons. In memory of this incident, the Jewish families are instructed to celebrate Pesach on the tenth day of the first month of the year by slaughtering a lamb and eating its meat with unleavened bread.[42] The blood of the lamb is to be daubed on the doorpost and lintels of their homes.

In a popular lecture available in YouTube, David Brickner, the executive director of an organization called *Jews for Jesus*, articulates the story and symbolism associated with each aspect of this sacred ritual:[43] *Z'roah*, the shank bone of a lamb, now replaces the Passover lamb, reminding the Jewish people that true sacrifice cannot be performed as long as the Jerusalem Temple remains destroyed. In the

Seder plates there are green leaves (*karpas*) dipped in salt water, symbolizing life soaked in tears; bitter herbs (*maror*) reminding them of the intense suffering during slavery; a mix of apple and honey (*charoset*) representing the mortar they worked with in Egypt; bitter root (*chazeret*) symbolizing the bitterness that lies hidden at the root of life itself; and a hardboiled egg (*chagigah*) representing the temple sacrifice.[44]

The Passover traditionally involves a mysterious custom in which the *matzo*, the unleavened bread, is kept in a *matzo tosh*, a linen bag with three compartments. During the celebrations the matzo from the middle compartment is taken out and broken in half. These broken pieces are wrapped in a linen cloth and hidden in a secret place until the end of the celebration. The hidden matzo becomes *afikoman*, or "that which comes after." At the end of the meal, children do a ceremonial search for afikoman. Once found, it is broken into smaller pieces for everyone in the house to eat.

Matzo is pierced and striped during the production process to facilitate the baking of the flour.[45] To Brickner, this texture of the unleavened bread symbolizes the striped and pierced body of Jesus Christ.

The three matzo pieces in the tosh represent the unity of the triune God (the Father, the Son, the Holy Spirit), out of which the middle piece (the Son) is taken out, broken, and buried for a while until it is "resurrected" again. In the end, this broken bread becomes the meal that brings eternal life to everyone.[46]

The New Testament clearly affirms Jesus as the Passover lamb sacrificed once for all.[47] Jesus validated this symbolism at his last meal: "This is my body, which is given up for you," he said, attributing a new meaning to the Passover meal. "This is my blood of the new covenant, which is shed . . . unto the forgiveness of sins."[48]

In the original Passover meal, one had to take the blood of the lamb and sprinkle it, first on the top lintel of the front door and then on the two side posts. In doing so, they inadvertently formed a sign of the cross, the ultimate sacrifice represented by the Passover lamb.

The priestly codes in Leviticus prescribe the blood of an animal a requirement for the atonement of sins. The act of sacrifice denotes a process of substitution, where the offered animal is enduring the punishment the offerer rightfully deserves.

Sacrifice brings reconciliation between God and the sinner, thus bringing humanity closer to God. The Hebrew term for sacrifice originates from the word korban, which literally means "to come close."[49]

The symbolism of atonement is portrayed even more vividly in the festival of Yom Kippur (the Day of Atonement).[50] On the day of this Jewish festival, two goats are sacrificed for the redemption of the entire nation. The first goat dies for the sins of the children of Israel, and its blood sprinkled on the Mercy Seat in the Holy of Holies, the innermost sanctum of the Temple. The second goat is released into the wilderness after the high priest transfers the sins of the nation symbolically upon its head. This goat wanders in the wilderness, bearing the sins of the people, and is eventually eaten by wild beasts.

Today the Jews believe that teshuvah (penitence) is the only thing that is necessary for atonement. "At the present times when the Temple no longer exists, and we have no altar for atonement, nothing is left but teshuvah," says Maimonides. "Teshuvah atones for all transgressions."[51] However, according to Mishna, the codified oral traditions of Judaism, teshuvah atones only for minor sins, and "if a serious sin has been committed it hangs in suspense until Yom Kippur comes and atones."[52] In other words, repentance is an integral part of the sacrifice, but it is not enough on its own to atone for sins.

The animal sacrifices we see in the Hebrew Scriptures, according to Christian theology, are foreshadows of the ultimate atoning sacrifice of Jesus Christ.[53] As the blood of a lamb covers the sins of the Jewish people, the blood of a sinless Messiah cleanses the whole world from its sins. Jesus' sacrifice on the cross fulfills the symbolic sacrifices in the Hebrew Scriptures. He identifies with both sacrificial goats (or lambs) of Yom Kippur— the lamb that was "slain from the foundation of the world," and "the lamb that bears the sins of the world."[54]

Jesus is our Passover lamb. His blood is what atones our sins on the day of Yom Kippur. He is the Messiah who once came into the world as a suffering servant, and he is going to come back again as the triumphant king.

The Jewish people may not yet see Jesus as such, but they have shepherded the tradition heralding his coming from time immemorial up until the present day. They have persisted through centuries of persecution, and they continue to wait in hope for the Messiah, both in Israel and in all of the countries to which they have been scattered.

There are still a few Jews remaining in Kochi. Although no one gathers at the synagogue anymore, they continue to make their presence felt in the religious landscape of my college town. Each time I visit Kochi I take a drive through the Jewish town. I utter a silent prayer for the Jews all over the world, reflecting on what Leo Tolstoy once said: "He who has been for so long the guardian of prophecy, and who transmitted it to the rest of the world, such a nation cannot be destroyed. The Jew is everlasting as is eternity itself."[55]

In the treasure chest of prophecy the Jews so carefully guarded, the Wise Men found God's best gift to humanity. The Star of the Savior that guided them is still lingering on the horizon, illuminating the prophetic visions of a universal Messiah.

We are almost there.

THE EMPTIED GOD

"Christ Jesus, who, although He existed in the form of God, did not regard equality with God a thing to be grasped, but emptied Himself... Being found in appearance as a man, He humbled Himself by becoming obedient to the point of death, even death on a cross."

Philippians 2: 5-8

I am an avid fan of Bono, the lead singer of the legendary band U2. I admire not only what he does, but also who he is. What captivates me the most is not his musical talent (impressive as it is); it is his uncanny ability to frame complex theological insights into everyday language. Listen to the following comments he once made to an interviewer:

> Christ says: No. I'm not saying I'm a teacher. Don't call me teacher. I'm not saying I'm a prophet. I'm saying: "I'm the Messiah." I'm saying: "I am God incarnate." ... So what you're left with is: either Christ was who He said He

was—the Messiah—or a complete nutcase. This
man was strapping himself to a bomb, and had
"King of the Jews" on his head, and, as they were
putting him up on the Cross, was going: OK,
martyrdom, here we go. Bring on the pain![1]

As absurd as it sounds, I am amused by his rendering of C. S.
Lewis' famous "trilemma theory" with such simplicity and
levity.[2] If Jesus is not Lord, he is either a liar or lunatic. If he
is not God, he is either bad or mad. If Christ is not worthy of
worship, he is worthy of no respect.

Jesus is a paradox, much like a rock star who preaches
theology in the mosh pit.

"Who do people say the son of man is?" Jesus asked his
disciples once.[3]

He often described himself by that title—the "son of man,"
a term in contemporary language that may sound
something like "average Joe."[4]

Jesus was not born a prince like Buddha; neither was he a
warrior like Muhammad. Statistically speaking, his life
seemed just as insignificant as most of us who live on this
planet. He was born into a working class family in an
obscure village, and lived most of his life as a blue-collar
construction worker. He did not even have formal
education, and most of his acquaintances were uncultured
country folks or social misfits—fishermen, tax collectors,
prostitutes, and the like.

The founder of the largest religion in the world was truly
an average Joe.

His disciples couldn't help but notice, however, that there
was something special about their Master. Unlike the other

teachers who speculated on abstract theories, he spoke about absolute truths with clarity and authority. He also performed many signs and wonders in front of their eyes. More importantly, his mother told them that she conceived him without any human contact. If that is the case, he must have been something more than just another man.

Some of the bizarre statements Jesus made about himself also stood out in their minds. A group of Jews were once bragging about how proud they were of their patriarch Abraham. Jesus looked them straight in the eyes and said, "Before Abraham was, I am."[5]

What he said sounded wrong on so many levels. It was grammatically incorrect to begin with. Instead of using the verb "I was" in past tense, Jesus said "I am," which happened to be a title reserved exclusively for God in the Jewish tradition. When God revealed Himself to Moses in a burning bush a few centuries before, He introduced Himself, "I am that I am."[6]

It was no secret that Jesus addressed the God of Moses as his "Father." Jesus also claimed that he came from heaven to do the will of his Father, and that he was going back to his Father's house where he had built many mansions for his followers. But when his followers asked who this Father was, he made another outrageous comment:

"He who has seen me has seen the Father."[7]

They scratched their heads. How could the Father and the Son be the same person? Had Jesus made a mistake?

"I and the Father are one," reiterated Jesus.[8]

This was a shocking—even blasphemous—claim. And yet it was not only what Jesus said that amazed his disciples the most; some of what he did also appeared far too outlandish.

One day, a group of friends brought a paralytic man to Jesus. They knew Jesus was going to heal him, of course. But just before healing him, Jesus proceeded to do an unimaginable thing. He proclaimed that the sins of the paralytic man were forgiven. How could he do such a thing? Forgiving someone's sins is a prerogative exclusively within the purview of God. Not even the High Priest had the authority to absolve sins. How then could a wandering teacher, who did not even belong to the priestly tribe, do so?

"Why does this man speak blasphemies like this?" people murmured. "Who can forgive sins but God alone?"[9] The disciples might have suspected at that point that the words and actions of their Master were bordering on the levels of insanity.

Bono and C. S. Lewis express the same concern using different vocabularies. Jesus can't be just another great teacher or prophet. He must have been a manipulative deceiver, or an eccentric blockhead. That is, unless he is . . .

"The Christ, the Son of the living God," as Peter, one of his disciples, put it.

***

The Son of God?

I hope Peter did not say it too loudly. It could have easily gotten him arrested for treason, even killed for that matter. There was only one person who could have been addressed as the "Son of God"—the Roman Emperor himself.

Everyone knew that the Romans considered their ruler to be God in human flesh. If Peter had taken a closer look at one of the coins in his pocket, he would have noted the inscription *Divi Filius* (Son of the Divine One) embossed on it. Julius Caesar was called the son of Zeus. Augustus Caesar was introduced as "son of a god, who shall restore the golden age and spread his empire."[10] The title "Son of God" was reserved exclusively for the emperor. It symbolized power, authority, and divinity. It was not a random title that could be ascribed to anyone, let alone a penniless preacher from a remote village in Palestine.

But to our surprise, Jesus did not correct Peter. We know he had to admonish Peter on many occasions for blurting out such infelicitous comments. But this was not one of them. "Blessed are you, Simon Barjona," said Jesus, "because flesh and blood did not reveal this to you, but My Father who is in heaven."[11] Instead of rebuking Peter, Jesus chose to applaud him. He described this discovery as some sort of divine revelation.

Authentic religion, this passage suggests, has to be a product of personal discovery. Peter had one such personal revelation here, and Jesus honored that. But Jesus then instructed the disciples not to reveal this truth to anyone. The discovery of Jesus' true identity is a matter of individual revelation, something outside the realm of mind and reason.

Christianity is a spiritual journey in the path of a progressive revelation. It starts with the knowledge of Jesus as the son of man, but advances slowly towards the realization of him as the Son of God.

Peter was well ahead of the curve in this journey. Another disciple, John, also known as the "one whom Jesus loved," progressed even further. He got to "see" Jesus, as he truly is—beyond this temporal world, in his heavenly glory. In the maddening loneliness of a solitary confinement on the island of Patmos, years after Jesus had been taken back up to heaven, the "Son of God" appeared to John. This is how he describes this indescribable event:

> In the middle of the lampstands I saw one like a son of man, clothed in a robe reaching to the feet, and girded across His chest with a golden sash. His head and His hair were white like white wool, like snow; and His eyes were like a flame of fire. His feet were like burnished bronze, when it has been made to glow in a furnace, and His voice was like the sound of many waters. In His right hand He held seven stars, and out of His mouth came a sharp two-edged sword; and His face was like the sun shining in its strength. When I saw Him, I fell at His feet like a dead man. And He placed His right hand on me, saying, "Do not be afraid; I am the first and the last, and the living One; and I was dead, and behold, I am alive forevermore, and I have the keys of death and of Hades.[12]

Jesus is just as divine as he was human. Although he appeared in the body of the son of man, his true essence is that of the Son of God.

***

How can a person be perfectly human and perfectly divine at the same time? It sounds like an oxymoron. Perhaps Jesus was a demigod, 50 percent man and 50 percent God?

Historically speaking, Jesus was born and raised in a modest Jewish family in the first-century in Palestine. But Christians (and, as we have seen, also Muslims) believe that his mother was still a virgin when he was conceived in her womb. He grew up as a normal child by all accounts, but the process of his birth was far from what can be considered "normal."

We don't know much about Jesus' life until he turned thirty. This is when we see him again as an itinerant preacher, proclaiming the arrival of "the kingdom of God," a spiritual domain in which God rules as the sovereign King.

Jesus' teaching was self-authenticating. It was its own authority. But the political leaders of the time charged him with insurrection. Ironically, the man who was born a peasant was executed with a sign that read "King of the Jews" nailed to his cross, and a crown of thorns upon his head.

But in this story, death was only the beginning. On the third day after his burial, Jesus came back to life. His resurrection, Christians claim, is the proof of a cosmic victory he won against the kingdom of darkness. His final triumph is yet to come, however. Christians (and Muslims) are eagerly waiting for his "second coming," when he is going to establish the kingdom of God for all eternity.

Jesus, in his death and resurrection, showed himself to be both true God and true man. But his "hybrid identity" was always a controversial and disputed topic. Indeed, the question of how to understand Jesus' simultaneous human and divine natures sharply divided Christians in the first few centuries following his ascension.

One faction known as the Arians, the disciples of Bishop Arius in the third century, believed that Jesus was neither fully God nor fully man. He was rather an in-between being, a lesser god or a higher man. God created him in the beginning, the Arians claimed, and then appointed him to do the rest of the creation. He was later assigned to save humanity from their sins, for which he will be rewarded with sovereign authority over the world.

"That is preposterous!" said another group, called Monophysites. "He was fully divine, and only appeared to be human." The Monophysites believed that Jesus' body was made of celestial substances, which created an illusion of flesh and blood. He was never born, lived, or died; what the people saw was nothing but an apparition. Jesus of Nazareth (the son of man) was an illusion created by the Cosmic Christ (the Son of God).

"You mean God tricked us with a phantom?" scoffed the Nestorians, followers of Bishop Nestorius. For them, Jesus' humanity was the most important reality. Jesus was first and foremost an ideal man who lived an exemplary life, which stands as a perfect model for all of humanity to follow. His divinity ensued as a result of his perfect life; it was something that enveloped his humanity like a halo. God invaded the body of Jesus of Nazareth so that He—God— could experience true humanity. The divinity of Christ possessed the humanity of Jesus to accomplish a specific mission.

Another group called Adoptionists took the middle ground. Jesus was an ordinary human for the first thirty years of his life, they speculated. But at the time of his baptism, God adopted him as His son. The son of man suddenly became the Son of God. But then God abandoned him on the cross. His divine nature evaporated and the human nature was restored while he suffered and died. On the cross, the Son of God became the son of man once again.

These disputes on the true identity of Jesus tore the Church apart into deeply divided factions. Church fathers, for centuries, desperately tried to articulate how human and divine elements coexisted in Jesus' being. "He alone is both God and man, and the source of all our good things," wrote Clement of Alexandria.[13] "The origins of both his substances display him as man and as God," argued Tertullian. "From the one, born, and from the other, not born."[14] Origen declared, "although he was God, he took flesh; and having been made man, he remained what he was: God."[15] Though the arguments were nuanced, the implications were profound, as each group accused the others of heresy and blindness to the true nature of Christ.

The schism continued in the Church until the Council of Nicaea in 325 CE declared Jesus as "God of God, Light of Light, very God of very God . . . being of one substance with the Father."[16] With this claim, the Church was affirming that Jesus was both fully human and fully divine—his divinity was identical to that of the God whom he called "the Father."

The Council of Chalcedon (451 CE) expanded upon this, proposing the "hypostatic" union between God and Jesus, in which "the human and divine natures of the Person of Christ co-exist, yet each remains distinct."[17] The Athanasian Creed likewise affirmed, "though he is God and Man, yet he is one Christ, not two, and he became man not by changing his deity to humanity, but by blending humanity with deity."[18] In other words, the identity of Jesus is a fusion of perfect humanity and perfect divinity.

We have already established in Chapter 5 that Jesus is called the "Son" not in the sense that he is created by the Father. It is rather a theological metaphor that may seem complex to us, but would have made perfect sense to his immediate audience.

When people of first-century Palestine addressed Caesar as the Son of God, they did not mean that Zeus birthed Caesar. Instead what they meant was that Zeus and Caesar were one and the same being. The emperor was just as divine as he was human. In the same way, when Christians address Jesus as the Son, it does not mean that he was birthed by the Father or that he is in any way inferior to the Father. Instead, it affirms that both God and Jesus are one and the same being.

This is why the New Testament writers are very intentional in describing Jesus as the "begotten" Son of God.[19] "To beget is to become the father of; to create is to make," explains C. S. Lewis. "And the difference is this. When you beget, you beget something of the same kind as yourself. ... What God begets is God. Just as what man begets is man. What God creates is not God. Just as what man makes is not man."[20]

We are all sons and daughters of God in the sense that we are created by Him. But only Jesus is begotten of God. Only he shares God's DNA.

Jesus, in other words, is 100 percent human and 100 percent divine. But how does this math make sense?

***

Prophet Isaiah once had a spectacular vision of God, not unlike the one John, the disciple of Jesus, had of the Son of God. Isaiah saw God sitting on a lofty throne, with the train of His robe flowing through the temple court. The foundations of the temple shook as six-winged seraphim shouted His praises: "Holy! Holy! Holy!"[21]

Roughly six hundred years later, John retells this story in his gospel, but with an interesting twist.[22] In order to emphasize people's stubborn refusal to believe in Jesus, John quotes one of Isaiah's prophecies: "He has blinded their eyes and He hardened their heart, so that they would not see with their eyes and perceive with their heart."[23] This verse is picked straight from the scene of Isaiah's majestic vision. But the next statement John makes is even more interesting: "These things Isaiah said because he saw His glory, and he spoke of Him"—Him here referring to Jesus.

We know that the One who was featured in Isaiah's vision is none other than God Himself. But in John's account, it was Jesus who appeared to Isaiah. The writer of the gospel is looking at the same person the prophet had seen six centuries previously.

In another episode in the Bible, Moses waits behind a rock to see God with his naked eyes.[24] No one can look at the face of God and remain alive, but Moses gets to see God's "back" through a cleft in the rock. He interacts with this God on many occasions, and even receives a handwritten tablet from Him. Yet, the writer of the book of Hebrews says that Moses considered "the reproach of Christ (Jesus) greater riches than the treasures of Egypt."[25]

Moses lived almost fourteen centuries prior to the arrival of Christ. How could he bear the reproach of Christ? Was Christ the same being as the "I am that I am" that Moses had been serving faithfully throughout his life? Was the God Moses saw through the cleft of the rock actually Jesus himself?

It is quite audacious to suggest that the Hebrew God Yahweh and the Christian God Jesus are one and the same.

But it is precisely what these passages seem to do. John and the writer of the book of Hebrews are referring to the same entity that Isaiah and Moses wrote about in their respective books.

This is the reason Christians believe in the idea of a triune God—One who has three identities (*hypostases*) in one substance (*Ousia*). The One God exists in three consubstantial persons: the Father, the Son (Jesus Christ), and the Holy Spirit.

In the Trinitarian framework there is no logical disparity in assuming that the God who appeared to Moses, Isaiah, and other Hebrew saints was the same God who walked with Peter, John and other disciples in first-century Palestine. They are simply different personifications of the same triune God.

***

But if Jesus is God, why wouldn't he say it plainly? Why would he want to keep us guessing?

In order to answer this question, we need to understand the subversive nature of Jesus' mission. He was in the process of founding an "upside-down" religion where the earthly standards are reversed: the first will be last and the last will be first; whoever saves his life will lose it and whoever loses his life will gain it. He envisioned an inverted Kingdom that is "not of this world." The King of this "secret" domain will not walk around giving out his business cards to everyone; only his true subjects will recognize him. As I mentioned before, religion has to be a personal discovery.

On the other hand, it is also not true to say that Jesus never made public claim of his divinity. As we have already seen, he asserted on many occasions that he and the Father are one, and whoever has seen him has already seen the Father. His immediate audience recognized the avowal of equality with God in his voice, and took stones to throw at him. "You, being a man, make yourself out to be God," they cried out.[26] Jesus may not have shouted from the rooftop that he was God, but the clues he left for those who wanted to discover his divinity were not by any means subtle.

Jesus also displayed divine attributes only God would have possessed. The disciples affirmed on multiple occasions, "You know all things," clearly recognizing his omniscience.[27] John recollects, "Jesus knew from the beginning who they were who did not believe, and who it was that would betray Him."[28] He demonstrated his omnipresence in the healing of those who were physically at distant locations. Where two or three are gathered together in his name, he claimed, he would be "in their midst."[29] His omnipotence is manifested in the many miracles he performed, which included even raising a corpse four days after its burial. Jesus claimed in no uncertain terms: "All authority has been given to me in heaven and on earth."[30]

We also have many witnesses in the Scriptures who would gladly testify to his divinity:

ANGELS worshipped Jesus:

> When He again brings the firstborn into the world, He says, "And let all the angels of God worship Him." (Hebrews 1:6)

THE DEVIL "bowed down" before Jesus, revealing his true identity as the Son of God:

> Seeing Jesus from a distance, he ran up and bowed down before Him; and shouting with a loud voice, he said, "What business do we have with each other, Jesus, Son of the Most High God? I implore You by God, do not torment me!" (Mark 5:6)

PROPHETS described Jesus as the "mighty God" and "eternal Father":

> For a child will be born to us, a son will be given to us; And the government will rest on His shoulders; And His name will be called Wonderful Counselor, Mighty God, Eternal Father, Prince of Peace. (Isaiah 9:6)

DISCIPLES worshipped him, and addressed him as "Lord and God":

> And those who were in the boat worshiped Him. (Matthew 14:33)

> And they came up and took hold of His feet and worshiped Him. (Matthew 28:9)

> When they saw Him, they worshiped Him. (Matthew 28:17)

> And they, after worshiping Him, returned to Jerusalem with great joy. (Luke 24: 52)

> Thomas answered and said to Him, "My Lord and my God!" (John 20:28)

THE OTHERS who were outside the disciples' band also recognized his divinity and worshipped him:

> After coming into the house [the Magi] saw the Child with Mary His mother; and they fell to the ground and worshiped Him. (Matthew 2:11)

> And [the man born blind] said, "Lord, I believe." And he worshiped Him. (John 9:38)

We know that only God is worthy of worship. If Jesus received worship from the angels, the devil, the disciples, and from everyone else, then his divinity requires no further proof.

According to the Scriptures, Jesus is "God manifested in the flesh," who is "the King eternal" and "the only God." He is also "the image of the invisible God" and "the exact representation of His nature." In Christ, "all the fullness of Deity dwells in bodily form."[31] Paul addresses him as the "great God," John describes him as "the true God," and Peter portrays him as "Our God and Savior."[32]

The verdict is loud and clear. Jesus of Nazareth is the personification of the almighty God, the most tangible expression of divinity we can ever aspire to witness. In him the transcendent God has become immanent, to whom we can relate like another human being.

***

A television comedian once mocked the God of Christians as a "single parent" who sent his only son on a "suicide mission."[33] This "space god" claims to love the world, the comedian notes, but instead of coming down to save it himself, he offers his son, who happens to be an innocent bystander!

I have to agree. From a worldly perspective, the Christian theory of atonement may sound that ludicrous. A big Father God pounding a smaller Son God to death on the cross. What a barbaric way to bring salvation to humanity!

The picture of God placing the burden of the sins of the world on His innocent son and then butchering him to death on the cross does not compute—unless, that is, we affirm the doctrine of Trinity. As we have already seen, the Christian God exists, and even suffers, in three distinct persons. If this is true, then Christ was not a victim of God's bloodthirsty rage, but "God was in Christ, reconciling the world to Himself."[34]

God did not send someone else to bear the burden of human salvation. The One that is hanging on the cross is God Himself.

We are now confronted with an even more important question. Why should someone have to die for the salvation of the world? Even if someone did, how could it be possible that one man's death could bring salvation to all of humanity?

The best way to answer this question is to use an often-quoted courtroom metaphor. Imagine yourself to be a judge, and a just one at that. One day a prisoner is brought in to your court. The moment your eyes fall on the defendant, you realize that it is your long-lost daughter. She ran away from home as a teenager, and you haven't heard from her ever since.

You hope the accusations now being leveled against her are false, and that she will be exonerated. You can't wait to get her shackles off, give her a big bear hug, and take her back home.

But unfortunately what happens is just the opposite. The jury finds the defendant guilty on all counts. They also emphasize the severity of her crime by recommending a death sentence.

All that remains now is for the judge to declare the verdict. If you are a just judge, your decision cannot be influenced by emotion. But you are also a loving father. There is no way you can pronounce a death sentence on your daughter.

This is an irreconcilable dilemma: As a just judge, you are obliged to sentence the defendant. But you are also a loving parent. You want to release her with impunity. The defendant may be guilty, but she is your child—you want to absolve her. How can you do both at the same time?

This is the dilemma God faces as He judges humanity. He is a just judge. A just judge is obliged to hold us accountable for all our actions. But we are fallen species. We are sinful, doomed to eternal separation from God, which, theologically speaking, is the ultimate death sentence.

The Christian God is not only a just judge but also a loving father. Importantly, I say "Christian God" because no other religion makes the astounding claim: "God is love."[35] God may be merciful, compassionate, or even "loving" in other religions, but in Christianity He is love itself.

What difference does it make? All the difference in the world! I am a loving person, but I am not love. I can "unlove" anyone anytime. But if God is love, He cannot choose to love whom and when He wants to love. He loves everyone all the time irrespective of their "lovability"—in fact, with God there is no one unlovable. Even His wrath is nothing but an expression of His love—intended for our ultimate good.[36]

If God loves us no matter what, can't He just forgive us? Of course He can. But if the loving God pardons sins at His will, He is no longer a just God. In other words, a just God cannot be love, and a God who is love cannot be just. Only one can prevail—either love or justice.

It is the ultimate catch-22: Our loving Father yearns to enter into a relationship with us. But our sinful nature makes us unworthy to face the just Judge that He is. This is what I call a heavenly dilemma. All religions stumble at this predicament. All they can do is to prescribe a series of penances and expiatory rituals to appease the just God, making religion a tiresome chore.

At this point in the Christian story, the unthinkable happens. The Judge comes down from the seat and bails out the defendant. He takes the death sentence on himself so that his child can walk free. The Judge dies in the place of the defendant to preserve the cosmic equilibrium between love and justice. Life emerges from death.

God experienced death in the humanity of Christ. The sins of the world were transferred onto Jesus, who took our place and received God's judgment. The law of God met the grace of God at his death. The love of God embraced the wrath of God on his cross. What a paradox!

God did not send someone else on a "suicide" mission. Instead He "emptied Himself" on the cross and performed the ultimate act of sacrifice necessary for the reconciliation of the world. In the cross of Christ, God ended religion and began a relationship.

***

"Who is this man?" asks Bono. "Was He who He said He was, or was he just a religious nut?"[37]

I too have wrestled with this question. Jesus made me choose between the extreme ends. There was no middle ground. Either he was the image of the invisible God or a disillusioned religious freak.

So here we are. Exactly where we started. A paradox. It is the first and the last word that comes to mind when I think of Jesus Christ.

Christ is a paradox: he is both human and divine at the same time; the Christian message is a paradox: "those who lose their life will find it and those who find their life will lose it"; the Christian life is a paradox: "when I am weak, then I am strong."[38]

Of course, when the infinite God invades the realm of the finite, it is bound to end up in a paradox.

Sylvia Dunstan, an alumnus of my seminary at the University of Toronto, sat down to ponder this paradox, and penned these beautiful verses:

> You, Lord, are both lamb and shepherd,
> You, Lord, are both prince and slave,
> You, peacemaker and sword-bringer,
> Of the way you took and gave.
>
> ......
>
> Worthy your defeat and victory.
> Worthy still your peace and strife.
> You, the everlasting instant;
> You, who are our death and life.[39]

I cannot even begin to comprehend the profundity of the paradox Sylvia was trying to capture in these poignant verses. I wonder if she could either. But she does know it now. Not soon after writing these verses, Sylvia entered a world where all the paradoxes metamorphose into a single truth—a person who claimed himself to be "the way, the truth, and the life."

Sylvia was only thirty-eight when she died of liver cancer. Her poem has since become one of my favorite hymns.

Jesus is a mystery as God Himself is. A mystery cannot be explained, but it can certainly be explored and experienced. Perhaps the best way to explore a paradox is to experience it for oneself.

It is the first and the foremost lesson I learned from the Wise Men. They embarked on an adventurous expedition from the East to the West in search of the greatest mystery ever revealed to humankind. The long and arduous journey brought them to a ramshackle barn in an isolated corner of the world. There they discovered, tucked inside a heap of straw, clinging to the bare chest of a woman—an emptied God, the ultimate paradox!

THE ONLY WAY

"The story of Christ is simply a true myth: a myth working on us in the same way as the others, but with the tremendous difference that it really happened."

"In Christ whatever is true in all religions is consummated and perfected."[1]

C. S. Lewis

We have been following the footsteps of the Wise Men on a trail that runs far and wide through countries, cultures, and religions. In this spiritual journey from the East to the West we came across many "Christ-figures" who bear close resemblance to the Jesus of the Bible. In the Hindu pantheon we encountered the avatar, an embodied god with a salvific mission. In the Buddhist universe we met the bodhisattva, an enlightened teacher who has taken the vow to rescue humanity from a suffering world. In Sikhism we witnessed God revealing Himself to the world through His Word. We came face to face with the Jesus of Islam, the only human ever to enter the world without a father and the only prophet who is going to come back again to reestablish God's domain on the earth. We explored the Jewish texts which struggle to reconcile the conflicting portrayals of the Messiah as a triumphant king and as a suffering servant. God's redemptive plan for the world has been unfolding in every culture and in every religion since the beginning of time.

We are now at a crossroad. We have two possible hypotheses to explain the presence of these Christ-figures in world religions, each leading to dramatically different conclusions.

The first hypothesis is termed the "Christ myth theory," according to which Christians fabricated the Jesus story, or at least doctored it, based on various pagan myths already available in other cultures. Jesus was not a historical figure, but a cosmic symbol that represents every man and woman; his life symbolizes the divine and human natures God has infused in all of us. This "Cosmic Christ" resides in our humanity, waiting to be actualized into divinity.

The second hypothesis suggests that God has intentionally implanted a version of the Christ myth in every religion and culture, hoping it would prepare the world for the arrival of the real Christ in the fullness of time. In other words, God revealed His plan of redemption to the Gentile world in symbolic forms, which would one day point them to the real redeemer—Jesus of Nazareth, in whom all Christ-figures find their historical fulfillment.

C. S. Lewis, in the same vein, argued that the person of Christ does not stand in opposition to the heroes of mythology; he is rather the historical culmination of what these myths were foreshadowing. "We must not be nervous about 'parallels' and 'pagan Christs,'" claimed Lewis. "They ought to be there."[2] Christianity, according to him, is a "true myth"—a cosmic story that became a historical reality. The sublime pictures of the redeeming savior we saw in other religions are secret codes God had programmed into their sacred narratives in order to prepare them for the arrival of His Son. Therefore "in Christ whatever is true in all religions is consummated and perfected."[3]

As a Christian, I embrace the second hypothesis—looking at Jesus as the historical manifestation of primordial truths God has engraved in every religion and culture. Scholars have long observed patterns of thoughts instinctual to all humanity, which influence and even shape our cultural narratives—be it philosophy, art or religion. Carl Jung, one of the founding fathers of modern psychology, called them "archetypes of the collective unconscious."[4] Jung argued that there are "primordial images" ingrained in every human psyche, which manifest themselves as archetypal characters in cultural myths across the world. The Christ-figures we observed in other religions could in fact be different versions of the Christ-archetype God has embedded in the sub-conscious of humanity.

***

Don Richardson, a missionary from Canada, travelled to Indonesia in the early 1960s with his wife and their six-month-old child. Their mission was to preach the gospel to the indigenous Sawi tribe of West Papua.

There was one problem, however. The Sawi were cannibalistic headhunters of the jungle who preyed on anyone that came across their path.

When they disembarked the boat and stepped onto the island, the Richardsons probably thought their story might end right there. But the Sawi people extended them a warm welcome. It is not uncommon for cannibals to use trickery and deception to befriend their victims. Was this reception part of one such nefarious scheme?

No, it turned out; the Sawi genuinely accepted the Richardsons into their community. It was an unexpected turn of events, and it took a while for them to figure out why their fate changed so dramatically.

When they entered the village with an infant child in their hands, the Richardsons were unknowingly becoming part of a tribal ritual—one that symbolized friendship and peace in the Sawi community. Whenever battles broke out between two villages, a man from one village would walk over to the enemy territory, carrying his son in his hands, and present him as an offering of peace. If the village chose to adopt the child and raise him as one of their own, there would be reconciliation between both parties. The child thus became a symbol of peace in the midst of war, and was named "the peace child."

As they learned of this tradition, the Richardsons were struck by its parallel to the gospel narrative. In order to restore the broken relationship between God and humanity, God walks into the enemy territory with His only Son as a peace offering. Isn't the story of the peace child, they wondered, an allegory of the Jesus story itself?

Jesus is our Peace Child. If we accept him, there will be peace and reconciliation between us and God.

The Richardsons used the peace child as an analogy to communicate the gospel to the Sawis. The rest is history. Today there is a thriving Christian community in the West Papua Island, which continues to cherish the eternal peace they found in the ultimate Peace Child.

After this episode, Don Richardson unearthed many "hidden clues" God has placed in different cultures that point people to His salvific plan for the world. Richardson calls them "redemptive analogies," which are essentially "aspects of a people's own culture, which contribute to the redemption of that people."[5]

Richardson has since observed traces of a monotheistic belief system at the very heart of primitive cultures around the world. Most ancient religions, Richardson argues, promote a belief in an omnipotent "sky god." In China, He is called *Shang Ti*, the Lord of Heaven, and in Korea He is *Hananim*, the Great One. The resemblance of this sky god to the God of the Bible is of particular interest to Richardson. After doing years of fieldwork and data analysis, he concludes: "One of the amazing characteristics of this 'sky god' . . . is His propensity to identify Himself with the God of Christianity."[6]

This discovery points us to a renewed understanding of the pattern of God's revelation to humankind. What if the savior figures in other religions are God's way of responding to the spiritual yearning of truth-seekers in every religion and in every culture? What if the mythological archetypes programmmed into our collective unconscious are precursors of a coming Savior? The promise of salvation woven into the sacred scriptures of world religions might have finally found its fulfillment in the person of Jesus Christ.

***

According to classical theology, there are two separate streams of revelation: "general revelation," through which God makes His presence felt in the universe, and "particular revelation," where God makes His salvific plan for the world known in Jesus Christ. General revelation is available to anyone with a seeking mind and a listening heart, but particular revelation comes only through the providential grace of God.

Let us picture God as the proverbial "man upstairs," hiding in an attic. He exists in a reality above our material world, separated by an impassable ceiling. But suppose He chooses to make a crack in the ceiling and lets His glory shine into the world. As the light of His revelation falls from the attic to the floor, it dissipates through the air at varying levels of intensity.

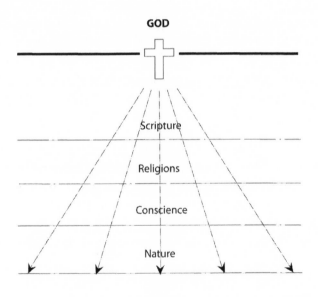

Figure 1

General Revelation

At the lowest level, God makes Himself known to the world through His "fingerprints" ingrained in the created universe. "The heavens are telling of the glory of God; and their expanse is declaring the work of His hands," sings the

Psalmist.[7] The beauty of nature and the wonders of creation invoke the presence of God in human spirit. Although God remains largely invisible to the material world, He has not left us "without witness." He manifests His benevolence by providing "rains from heaven and fruitful seasons, satisfying our hearts with food and gladness."[8]

In the next level up, the light of general revelation is reflected in our conscience. When we confront a moral choice, for example, an "inner voice" prompts us to a particular direction, often against our own self-interest. When we do something wrong, we are haunted by a "guilty conscience," and when we make it right we enjoy a "clear conscience." The conscience thus becomes our moral DNA, functioning as God's law "written on our hearts."[9] In the absence of an absolute written law, it allows us to become "a law to ourselves" by providing an inherent ability to discern between right and wrong.[10]

One level higher up, God's revelation is manifested in the many religions of the world, most of which possess at least a partial understanding of the One true God. Religions are essentially products of human search for God, and their sacred writings emerge from our insatiable quest for the ultimate truth. Therefore, it is natural to assume that all religions possess the power to produce genuine spiritual experiences at varying intensities.

The Roman Catholic Church was quick to observe and appreciate the light of God's revelation in other religious traditions. "The Catholic Church rejects nothing that is true and holy in these religions," says Nostra Aetate. "She regards with sincere reverence those ways of conduct and of life, those precepts and teachings which, though differing in many aspects from the ones she holds and sets forth, nonetheless often reflect a ray of that Truth which enlightens all men." It is important to note, however, that the centrality of Jesus Christ is of paramount importance to the Catholic creed. Jesus is the one "in whom men may find the fullness of religious life, in whom God has reconciled all things to Himself."[11]

Today even the most conservative theologians recognize and acknowledge the presence of God's redemptive revelations in other religions. Amos Yong, a leading voice of modern Evangelicalism, argues that the Holy Spirit is at work in other religions, and for this reason, "the religions of the world, like everything else that exists, are providentially sustained by the Spirit of God for divine purposes."[12] Such a belief does not lead us to universalist pluralism, but it only recognizes the activity of God's Spirit in unexpected places.

It should be remembered, however, that each religion frames God's revelation through its own theological filter. In this process, the message does get skewed or corrupted. Paul says that in the "foolishness of their wisdom," people abrogate the infinite God into finite forms, thus becoming "futile in their speculations." They are able to see the source of revelation only through broken and dusty glasses.

The highest level of revelation available to humanity today, according to Christianity, is the Scripture. The Bible is "God-breathed" (*theopneustos*), and therefore it is both infallible and inerrant.[13] It is called "the word of God" because it is the best expression of God's mind in written form. Through the Bible we receive the clearest and the most intimate picture of who God is and what He desires in the world.

In summing up, general revelation is like a ray of light, filtered through multiple lenses of different focal lengths. The light from the attic is reflected at various intensities—in nature, in human conscience, and in world religions; and even more brightly in the Bible. Each level projects different images of God—big, small, stretched, or skewed. In the end, each tier of revelation reflects only part of the fullness of God; His ultimate "self-disclosure" happens at the attic ceiling, in Jesus Christ, who is "the image of the invisible God."[14]

God has chosen to reveal Himself to the world at different levels, in varying degrees of opacity. But in the end, He wants to draw us all into the culmination of His revelation in Jesus Christ. To accomplish this purpose, I believe, He has cast the shadows of His salvific plan in the sacred writings of world religions. In Jesus Christ, these shadows turn to light, and God draws the whole world into the very source of the light itself.

***

The English poet William Blake coined the phrase "*All religions are one*," which has since become a cultural meme in our conversations about faith and spirituality. It is an honest statement often made by well-meaning folks, but I, for one, find it logically inconsistent and factually untrue.

Let us look at a familiar example: All political parties strive towards the same goal—peace and prosperity of the nation. But have you ever heard someone say, "All parties are one; it doesn't matter who you are voting for?" Of course not. We know that even though all parties share similar aspirations, each of them proposes its own exclusive route to our political destiny.

Religion, like politics, has often been a divisive force in the history of humanity. So, frankly, I would also like to say "all religions are one," at least for the sake of finding unity in the midst of our diversity. But unfortunately, in my research on world religions, I found the opposite to be true. Although all religions promise to take us to the same destination, each of them travels in diametrically different directions.[15]

After completing an extensive analysis of eight world religions, Steven Prothero, a professor of religion at Boston University, concludes: "The world's religious rivals do converge when it comes to ethics, but they diverge sharply on doctrine, ritual, mythology, experience, and law. These differences may not matter to mystics or philosophers of religion, but they matter to ordinary religious people."[16] Even if we try to downplay these differences for the sake of political correctness or religious tolerance, the inevitability of the truth will eventually catch up to us at some point.

World religions, I believe, are fundamentally "exclusivist" at their heart. Jehovah, the Jewish God, insists that there is no God beside Him.[17] Christianity credits its religious heritage to Judaism, but it promotes the idea of a Triune God—a fatal heresy in the eyes of its parent religion. Islam alleges that both Jews and Christians are "deluded away from the truth" and condemns them to "God's curse."[18] The Quran even cautions Muslims from having Jewish or Christian friends, as they are "forbidden from the Garden," and destined to end up in the fires of hell.[19]

The claim of exclusivity resides at the theological center of the Christian faith as well. Jesus stated unequivocally, "No one comes to the Father but through me."[20] It sounds like an intolerant statement, and my first instinct is to somehow explain it away. But then comes Peter, Jesus' chief of staff, reiterating the claim even more fiercely. "There is salvation in no one else," said Peter. "For there is no other name under heaven that has been given among men by which we must be saved."[21]

It is the simple truth. Despite all our attempts to present it in a politically correct package, the gospel of Jesus Christ is unapologetically exclusivist.

I now find myself in a precarious position. By virtue of my upbringing in India, most of my friends are either Hindus or Muslims. They are good people of noble character. As a matter of fact, I trust them just as much as, if not more than, some of my Christian friends. I cannot imagine the possibility of them being cast out from the presence of God simply because they did not follow my religion.

The second hypothesis we discussed earlier might suggest a way out of this predicament.

The Bible unequivocally claims that there is only one way to God, and that way is Jesus, but does it insist that there is only one way to Jesus?

There are over forty-five thousand Christian denominations in the world, most of which claim to be exclusive ways to approach the one Jesus.[22] What if there is another way—or ways— to Jesus that we are unaware of?

Read it carefully. I am not saying that there is more than one way to God. If I were, I would certainly be contradicting the Bible. But if I say there could be more than one way to Jesus, I might only be challenging a loosely held Church dogma, not the Bible itself.

Of course, different religions claim to provide different ways "to" God. But only Christianity introduces a way "from" Him. "I have come down from heaven," said Jesus.[23] No religious leader has ever dared to make such an audacious claim.

The teachers and prophets of other religions promise to take us to places they themselves have never been before. But only Jesus can lead us to the presence of God, because that is exactly where he came from. Only the One who descended from God can help us ascend to Him.

What if there is more than one way "to" Jesus, who is the only way "from" God?

Figure 2

The Only Way

If it is true, Jesus stands at the intersection between God and world religions. In him, God's plan of redemption is perfected as the many ways "to" God meet the only way "from" Him.

Make no mistake: I do not believe in universal salvation, nor do I condone a worldview in which everything is subjective and relative. As a Christian, I affirm that any religion that does not recognize God's self-disclosure in Christ, no matter how honest and benevolent it might be, cannot function as a direct path to God.

This conviction, however, does not prevent me from acknowledging God's (general) revelation different religions possess in different measures, as their sacred scriptures artfully depict many silent pointers to the only way from God. When I am sharing the gospel with my neighbors of other faiths, therefore, I am not selling them a new religion; I am only introducing them to a person who embodies the fullness of their own religious expectations.

Jesus Christ was not a messenger from God; he was the message. The Gospel is not merely a truth-claim; it is the truth personified.

The Christian message is a living, breathing entity.

***

Jesus came into this world to prove that God is not a racist.

In him, the many faces of the Christ-figure we observed in different religions crystalized and manifested in history. The grace of God that brings salvation appeared to "ALL men."[24] It is the "good news of great joy," meant for "ALL people."[25]

This is the lesson I learnt from the story of the Wise Men. The savior's birth was for the East and the West. He established His kingdom for the Jews and the Gentiles. God does not play favorites. There is a broad spectrum of inclusivity within the exclusivity of His gospel.

While in seminary, I heard Karl Barth, arguably the most brilliant theologian of the twentieth century, pondering on "God's strange voice outside the walls of Christianity."[26] Barth believed that Christ's death was intended for all men, and he could indeed reconcile all the world to the Father if he chose to do so. "I do not preach universal salvation," Barth insisted. "What I say is that I cannot exclude the possibility that God would save all men at the Judgment."[27]

In the same vein, Karl Rahner, an eminent Catholic theologian, suggested that people could be saved by the salvific work of Jesus Christ even though they have never had an opportunity to know him personally or acknowledge their faith in him publicly. Rahner described them as "anonymous Christians"—Christians outside the Christian tradition.[28]

C. S. Lewis followed suit: "If you are a Christian you do not have to believe that all other religions are simply wrong all through," said Lewis. "There are other people who are being led by God's secret influence ... who thus belong to Christ without knowing it."[29]

All these ideas sounded like borderline heresy at the time. Were Barth and Rahner preaching a politically correct gospel where everyone reaches the same destination irrespective of the paths they have chosen? Did Lewis believe that all religions are essentially one and the same? Of course not. They were contemplating the possibility of people following Jesus without being consciously aware of the fact that they are following him.

Remember that boy in the blue shirt? Now I feel like I am with him on the stage, becoming part of God's unfolding magic act in this world. I look around to see "the others," watching us from the dark. I cannot see them, but I know they are there, and they play an important role in the act even though they do not realize it yet. As soon as the Magician takes a bow, all the lights in this cosmic theater will turn on, and the hidden witnesses will be revealed.

This truth hits home when I read the Rig Veda, the four-thousand-year-old Hindu sacred text. The silhouette of another Christ-figure emerges from behind the veils, seemingly pointing us to Paul's Mars Hill sermon all over again:

To the Unknown God
(Mandala X Hymn 121 Rig Veda)

In the beginning there arose the Golden Child
As soon as born, he alone was the lord of all that is.
He established the earth and this heaven:
Who is the God to whom we shall offer sacrifice?

He who gives breath, he who gives strength,
Whose command all the bright gods revere,
Whose shadow is immortality, whose shadow is death,
Who is the God to whom we shall offer sacrifice?

He who through his might became the sole king
Of the breathing and twinkling world,
Who governs all this, man and beast
Who is the God to whom we shall offer sacrifice? [30]

Who is this "unknown god" to whom the Hindu rishis were offering sacrifices? Did the *Agnestos Theos* of the Athenians present himself in other religions and cultures as well?

Many of my ancestors in India died without ever hearing about the God of the Bible through no fault of their own. But the Vedic poem seems to suggest that they could have been worshipping the one true God, not knowing that they were actually worshipping Him.

What if these outsiders come to realize that the unknown god they worship has already revealed himself in history through the person of Jesus Christ? What if they recognize the mystical truth that the one to whom they have been offering sacrifices has offered himself as the ultimate sacrifice for their salvation? What if they discover Jesus, like the Wise Men of the East, even through unorthodox ways? What good news would that be!

In the book of Revelation, we see Jesus knocking at the door of a human heart. The one who opens the door will dine with him.[31] As I read this passage, I cannot help but imagine a group of neighbors across the street, watching this man who is standing at my door. They see Jesus from different vantage points; it creates different perspectives of him in their mind. But the one who opens the door will get to see him for who he truly is.

What if the Christ at my door is visible to my neighbors of other faiths through the "windows" of their own religious traditions? What if God has allowed world religions to capture blurred visuals of the same Jesus who revealed himself more tangibly in the Christian faith?

If you are someone who has already opened the door to Jesus I hope my stories have helped you notice the others who are trying to catch a glimpse of him through the windows across the street. If you are one of those neighbors peering through the windows, I invite you to come to the door. Open it wide and see who he truly is!

One day, I believe, all of us will get to see him face to face. God will remove the "shroud that enfolds (all) the people, the sheet that covers all nations."[32] The whole world will see the apotheosis of the fragmented revelations that already exist in our midst, converging in the fullness of Jesus Christ. Until then, all we can do is to continue exploring these stories—the stories of the unknown followers of the unknown god.

EPILOGUE

My twelve-year-old self curls up inside the blanket, still listening to the Vedic chants seeping in through the bedroom window.

The Gayatri mantra has come to an end. The temple priest is now chanting another versatile prayer in lyrical Sanskrit:

> Asatho ma Satgamaya
> (Lead me from Delusion to Truth)
> Thamaso ma Jyothrigamaya
> (Lead me from Darkness to Light)
> Mruthyor ma Amrutham Gamaya[1]
> (Lead me from Death to Life)

The cone-shaped loudspeaker on top of the church-dome responds, almost intuitively:

> I am the Truth   (John 14:6)
> I am the Light   (John 8:12)
> I am the Life   (John 14:6)

A profound prayer receives a propitious answer.

The Supreme Light trickles in through the window, embracing me with its invisible arms. Its warmth and tenderness are comforting.

The Star that guided the Wise Men is still moving through the darkened sky beyond the horizon. Its shimmering rays radiate the "true Light which enlightens every man."[2]

I am waking up.

ABOUT THE AUTHOR

Mathew P. John considers himself a citizen of
the world. Originally an electrical engineer
from the East (India), he pursued a successful
corporate career in the Middle East (Kuwait),
and eventually transitioned from 'technology
to theology' in the West (Canada). He holds a
Master's degree in Theological Studies (MTS)
from the University of Toronto (Canada) and a
PhD in Intercultural Studies from Fuller Theological Seminary (USA). His dissertation won
the prestigious Alan Tippett Award for bringing three disciplines i.e. anthropology, world
religions, and world cinema into a trialogue.

Mathew is the creator of *The Mosaic Course*, an
online platform for exploring world religions
from a Christian perspective. He is also an
award winning producer and alumnus of the
Professional Producer's Program at UCLA
School of Theater, Film and Television.

Mathew has acquired over two decades of professional experience in various academic, corporate and ecclesiastical platforms. He has taught courses in theology, film, and culture, and presented papers at academic conferences hosted by the American Anthropological Association, Center for Religion at UCLA etc. He has also authored *Film as Cultural Artifact: Religious Criticism of World Cinema* (Fortress, 2017) and contributed essays to *God in Movies* (Brazos, 2017).

Mathew currently lives in Los Angeles with his wife, Joanne and their two daughters, Hannah and Emma. He may be contacted through the publisher:

author.mpj@focusinfinity.com

END NOTES

Chapter 1
FOLLOWING THE STAR

1. Miller, P. (1988*)*. *Kerala: Jewel of India's Malabar Coast* National Geographic National Geographic May
2. W.J., M. (1809). *The Lusiad or The Discovery of India* London, Allen and Co. Page 240
3. "According to Western church tradition, Balthasar is often represented as a king of Arabia, Melchior as a king of Persia, and Caspar as a king of India." Encyclopædia Britannica Online, s. v. "Magi", accessed May 24, 2016, http://www.britannica.com/topic/Magi.
4. The Magi are considered to be kings in their land.
5. Deuteronomy 14:2
6. The city of Cochin – More details about the Jewish connection of Cochin in Chapter 6
7. Genesis 12:2
8. Genesis 12: 18,19
9. Amos 3:2
10. Genesis 9:1-17
11. Isaiah 49:6
12. Isaiah 19: 19-25
13. Amos 9:7
14. Isaiah 56:7
15. Kaiser, W. C. (2012). *Mission in the Old Testament: Israel as a Light to the Nations*. Grand Rapids, Baker Academic. Page 32
16. Jonah 4:11
17. The Northern kingdom of Israel was destroyed by Assyrians in 722 BCE.
18. 2 Chronicles 35: 20 – 22
19. 2 Chronicles 35:22
20. Genesis. 14:19-20
21. One hypothesis suggests that Both El and Elyon were Canaanite names for Yahweh Himself.
22. Psalms. 110:4
23. Exodus 18:1-17
24. 2 Chronicles. 2: 3-16
25. 2 Chronicles. 36: 22-23
26. Mark 9: 38 – 40, Luke 9: 49, 50
27. John 10:16
28. John 15:16, Ephesians 1:4
29. Acts 10
30. 2 Peter3 :9
31. Romans 10: 12-13

32. 1 Timothy 4:10
33. Acts: 17:30
34. 1 Timothy 2:4
35. Isaiah 45:6
36. Matthew 5: 14
37. Acts 17:28
38. Encyclopaedia Britannica, Macropeadia, 15th ed., vol. 3, p. 924
39. Another excerpt from this poem "Cretans, always liars," is also quoted by Paul in Titus 1:12. The "lie" of the Cretans was that Zeus was mortal; Epimenides considered Zeus immortal.
40. Acts 17:22-34
41. Paul certainly knew the story behind the unknown God. He quotes Epimenides' poem not only in his sermon, but also later in his epistle to Titus (Titus 1:12) As a matter of fact, he addresses Epimenides not as a poet, but as a prophet. According to legends, it is Epimenides who initiated the cult of the unknown God.
42. Acts 17:22-34

Chapter 2
THE DESCENT OF GOD

1. Of the TV show *The Mindy Project* (NBC/Fox 2012-2015), among other acting credits.
2. Satya Nadella (CEO, Microsoft), Sundar Pichai (CEO, Google).
3. Miller, L. (2009). "We are all Hindus Now." *NewsWeek*. 31 Aug 2009.
4. "I'm a Hindu: Julia Roberts." *Times of India*. August 7, 2010. Retrieved 11/20/2016, 2016, from http://timesofindia.indiatimes.com/entertainment/english/hollywood/news/Im-a-Hindu-Julia-Roberts/articleshow/6265252.cms.
5. Gita 7:21,22
6. Rig Veda, 1.164. 46
7. Vivekananda, S. (1989). *The Complete Works of Swami Vivekananda Almora*, Advaita Ashrama, Page 19
8. Eight limbs of the Yoga (Ashtanga Yoga): *(1) Yama*: Five abstentions (DON'Ts): from injury, lying, stealing, sensuality, greed *(2) Niyama*: Five observances (DOs) : cleanliness, contentment, self-control, studiousness, contemplation of the divine. (3) *Asanas*: Eighty-four postures are mentioned in the text, intended to keep the body from distracting the mind while it concentrates. *(4)Pranayama*/Breathing: The mastery of respiration conducive to meditation. (5) *Pratyahara* / Contemplation: Focusing inward. The Yogi becomes alone with his mind. (6) *Dharmana* /Concentration: Focusing the mind protractedly on an object, in order to

exorcize thoughts from the subconscious. (The mind's fiercest antagonist is itself.) (7) *Dhyana*/Meditation: Concentration deepens to a stage where the mind loses consciousness of itself as an object distinct from the one it was focusing on. (8) Samadhi: A state in which human mind is completely absorbed in God. The mind attains the knowledge of the Absolute and has been dissolved into it. (It is also the term of death. Gurus don't die. They achieve Samadhi.)

9. I am sad to report that like many other film projects it also got lost in what the producers call "the development hell" and is yet to see the light of the day.

10. There are four sacred scriptures or Vedas in Hinduism: Rig, Yajur, Sama and Atharva. Among these Atharva Veda is considered forbidden to the uninitiated because it contains various kinds of black magic using the spirits of darkness.

11. Gita 6: 1

12. Gandhi is a classic example of a karma yogi. His political struggle was not pursuit of power, but he called it *Satyagrha,* which means 'the quest for truth.' There was always a spiritual undertone to all his outward actions.

13. Chandogya Upanishad VI.8.7

14. Brihad Aranyaka Upanishad, I. 4.10

15. Rig Veda, 10.82.2

16. Rig Veda, 10.81.3

17. His identity is not as static as the God of the Bible; in fact, Bhakti yoga believes that all personal deities are nothing more than Iswara representing Himself in different forms. A devotee is free to choose from among many gods appearing in the *puranas,* the collection of Indian mythologies.

18. Mahabharata Book 3. CCLXX page 531 (Sacred Text.com)

19. Brahma is the creator god with four heads that face all different directions. He is not worshipped by Hindus. Shiva is the lord of dance (*nata raja*) who sets the rhythm of the world. The world will end when he stops dancing. He often appears with his consort goddess Shakti, also a manifestation of the mother goddess. Vishnu sleeps over a cosmic ocean on a great serpent made up of the remains of the previous universe. His consort is goddess Lakshmi (fortune). Those who worship Shiva are called Shivites and those who worship Vishnu are Vaishnavites.

20. Gita 18:66 http://www.holy-bhagavad-gita.org/ (Compare it with Mathew 11:28 – "Come to me all you who are weary and heavy-laden.")

21. Gita11:44

22. Gita 18:66 http://www.holy-bhagavad-gita.org/

23. Dhavamony, Mariasusai. *Hindu-Christian Dialogue : Theological Sounding and Perspectives.* Amsterdam: Rodopi, 2002.

24. As I write this, his film *Avatar* (2009) is the highest grossing film with a reported revenue of over $2.7 billion

25. (1) Fish/matsya, which saved the world and Vedic texts from a primordial flood; (2) Tortoise/korma, which helped churning the ocean for amrurtham by supporting the mount on its back; (3) Boar/varaha, which

brought back the earth which was sinking to hell (patal lok) to its original position; (4) man-lion/narasimha, who saved his devotee Prahlada from the murder plot devised by his own furious father; (5) dwarf/vamana, who tricked king Mahabali to give up his kingdom; (6) Parasurama, who destroyed the enemies of the Brahmins, using a big axe; (7) Rama, a dutiful husband and king who fought a 1,000-headed demon to save his wife Sita; (8) Krishna, the charioteer who played a pivotal role in Kurukhestra Yudha; (9) Balarama, older brother of Krishna, a war hero who taught both sides of the warring faction the art of war but remained neutral in the war and (10) Kalkin, an avatar to appear at the end of this year. Not all avatars are full manifestations of His Godhead. There are the *nitya avatara*, the continual presence of God in the world (through the lives of saints and sages), the *amsha avatara*, a temporary disguise God uses to accomplish a specific task at a specific point in time, and the *poorna avatara*, the only perfect manifestation of God, who *is* Lord Krishna (or Lord Rama in another tradition).

26. Nathan, R. S., Ed. (1983). *Symbolism in Hinduism*. Bombay, Central Chinmaya Mission Trust. Page 116. Rama is Dharma (duty)- oriented, whereas Krishna is Karma (action)- oriented.

27. Chinmayananda, S. (1983). Radha and Krishna. *Symbolism in Hinduism*. R. S. Nathan. Bombay, Central Chinmaya Mission Trust. Page 112.

28. Jeremiah 31:20, John 3:29, 2 Corinthians 11:2, Revelation 19:7

29. Bhagavata Purana 2.7.38

30. Revelation 21:1-5

31. Schouten, P. J. (2008). *Jesus as Guru: The Image of Christ Among Hindus and Christians in India*. Amsterdam, Rodopi.

32. Bhagavad-Gita : IV: 7-8

33. Mark 2:17

34. Luke 19:10

35. Sarbatoare, O. "Yanja – Vedic Sacrifices in Hinduism." http://www.hinduwebsite.com/hinduism/vedicsacrifice.asp accessed on 10/31/2016

36. Rig Veda 10.121.10

37. It was not a permanent temple, but a residential building which is also used as an office. I was also told that it was part of a movement within Indian Christianity which wants to make Christian faith more 'indigenous.' Most Christians in India would consider such an attempt a 'heresy.' There are many Hindu-Christians who make these Prajapati- Christ connections. There are both arguments 'for' and 'against' it, yet it is part of an 'insider movement' in Hinduism.

38. Sathapatha Brahmana 10.1.3. 2

39. The myth of the primordial Adam, found in gnostic and essene. In the gnostic myth, there was said to have existed in the beginning of creation a spiritual body of light referred to as the primordial Adam (in gnostic Christianity). This primordial body was broken up by demonic forces into pieces of light, each piece becoming a soul to be born into the world. At

the end of time a redeemer was to come to "save" the souls of light, rejoining them into the great spiritual body.

40. Sathapatha Brahmana 11, 1; 8, 2
41. Satapathabrahmana 10.2.2.1-2
42. Brhadaranykopanisad 3.9.28.4,5
43. Sathapatha Brahmana 10.1.3.
44. "Taken in its totality, the myth of the Purusha/Prajapati is not unworthy of the Christian conception of the redemptive incarnation of the logos (Word = Jesus)" Augilar, H. (1976). *Sacrifice in the Rg Veda.* Delhi, Bharatiya Vidya Prakasham. Page 69.
45. Revelations 13:8

Chapter 3
THE SUFFERING SAVIOR

1. Yandell, K. and H. Netland (2009). *Buddhism: A Christian Exploration and Appraisal.* Downers Grove, Intervarsity Press. Page 41.
2. Episode 3 Season 4, "The Pitch."
3. Eckel, M. D. *Great World Religions: Buddhism.* The Learning Company.
4. Keown, D. (2013). *Buddhism: A Very Short Introduction.* Oxford, Oxford University Press. Page 53.
5. S*kandhas* are constantly shifting components that emerge out of a process called "dependent origination." There are five skandhas: physical body (*rupa*), sensation (*vedana*), perception (*samjna*), cognition (*sankhara*), and consciousness (*vijnana*).
6. Some scholars are not sure if Buddha was actually a historical figure because most of what we know about him comes from legends and mythologies passed on through oral tradition. We don't have the first written account of his life until Asvaghosha who compiled Buddha Charita (Life of Buddha) approximately 600 years after his time i.e. in the second century CE.
7. Keown, D. Page 38.
8. Ecclesiastes 1:1
9. Keown, D. Page 49.
10. Keown, D. Page 57.
11. A few may applaud this philosophy, as "it accepts life as it is." If so, one has to wonder: do we need the help of a religion to do so?
12. Ecclesiastes 12:13,14
13. 268–239 BCE
14. Muslim emperors considered Buddhists as idol worshippers because there were just as many statues in a Buddhist temple as in a Hindu temple. This is why a religion that is perceived as a harmless nontheistic philosophy is branded an idolatrous religion by the Islamic jihadists.
15. Keown, D. Page 139.
16. Buddhism, for this reason, is often described as the chameleon among world

religions. It has the capacity to morph into any shape or form depending on its environment—and indeed has done so at various times and in various locations throughout history.

17. The Message of Buddhism by Bhikkhu Subadhra as quoted in Lodge, B. (1929). *What is Buddhism?* London, Buddhist Lodge.

18. Eckel, M. D

19. Gomez, L. *The Land of Bliss: The Paradise of the Buddha of Measureless Light : Sanskrit and Chinese Versions of the Sukhāvatīvyūha.* University of Hawaii Press, 1996.

20. The current Dalai Lama is the fourteenth reincarnation of the original Dalai Lama.

21. Quoted by Keown, Page.121 from Humphreys' "Sixty Years of Buddhism in England," page 80.

22. Bodhisattvas are generally identified by six perceptions: generosity (dana), morality (sila), patience (ksanti), courage (virya), meditation (Samadhi), and wisdom (prajna).

23. Keown, D. Page 62.

24. Eckel, M. D.

25. Keown, D. Page 65.

26. 1506–1552 CE

27. Reeves, M. (2012). *Delighting in the Trinity: An Introduction to The Christian Faith.* Downer's Grove, IVP Academic.

28. 1133–1212 CE

29. Bary, W. T. d., et al., Eds. (2001). *Sources of Japanese Tradition: Volume 1.* New York, Columbia University Press. Pages 208-209.

30. Keown, D. Page 62.

31. It was chanted in different languages, but this is an approximate translation I found on the Internet. [http://terebess.hu/zen/szoto/vows.htm accessed on 12/18/2016].

32. Eckel, M. D.

Chapter 4
THE WORD BECOMES THE LORD

1. The Islamic emperors of India unleashed a series of vicious punishments against Sikhs considering them as heretic Muslims. One of the Sikh Gurus, Arjan Sing, was boiled in oil and then cut into pieces by the Islamic Mugal emperors of India.

2. Also called *Ek Omkar*, associated with the Hindu Om.

3. Only those who are members of the official Sikh community, *Khalsa*, need to follow the 5Ks. All Sikhs who are initiated into Khalsa are regarded equal, irrespective of their economic or social status. As a symbol of equality they share the same surname— Singh (lion) for male, and Kaur (princess) for female.

4. Gidoomal, R. and M. Wardell (1996). *Lions, Princesses, Gurus: Reaching Your Sikh Neighbour.* Highland. Page 69.

5. The Pew Research Center Report on World Religion classifies Sikhism in the "other" category, combining it with a number of eastern religions such as Confucianism or Taoism.This is primarily because Sikhism still remains largely as an ethnic religion, centered around the Punjab state of India.

6. Guru Nanak made sure that he appointed Gurus from outside his family circle. But after the second Guru, the title became a family heritage. The sixth Guru Har Govind was only nine years old when he assumed the title. The eighth Guru Har Kishan was only five, and he died of smallpox when he turned eight.

7. Guru Granth Sahib 1187-10.

8. Gidoomal, R. and M. Wardell. The text lays out a comparison of the Sat Guru and Jesus.

9. Gidoomal, R. and M. Wardell. Page 140-141.

10. Quoted in Ahmad, S. (1978). *Sikhism and Christian Faith.* Lucknow, Lucknow Publishing House. Page 118. (This is a secondary reference and I am not sure about the legitimacy of this source).

11. "Sri Guru Granth Sahib." SikhismGuide.org http://www.sikhismguide.org/granth.aspx accessed on 11/20/2016.

12. Christ's love for his people is often described as the love of a bridegroom for his bride (Ephesians 5:25; 2 Corinthians 11:2).

13. Please read her story in Scrivens, Mona. (2012) *Jesus According to Sikhism* Focus Infinity.

14. Singh, N. "Jesus through Sikh Eyes." BBC, October 26, 2009. http://www.bbc.co.uk/religion/religions/sikhism/people/jesus.shtml accessed on 11/11/2016.

15. This is a religious rite called "Akhand Path."

16. Guru Granth Sahib 1136:4

17. Guru Granth Sahib 943: 1

18. "In the beginning was the Word, and the Word was with God, and the Word was God. . . . The Word became flesh and made his dwelling among us." John 1:1, 1:14

19. John 1:1

20. John 1:14

Chapter 5
THE MAN WHO BECAME A SIGN

1. Trinity, according to Islam, is the worship of three different gods—forbidden in this monotheistic religion.

2. The Quran has only a total of 114 chapters (sura) and 6,666 verses.

3. Muhammad's father (Abdulla) died few days before he was born in 570 CE. His mother (Amina) died when he was around six. His grandfather who cared for Muhammad died when he was eight.

4. The first revelation (Sura 96:1-5) came in 610 CE and it continued until Muhammad's death in 632 CE.

5. Scholars note that there were many competing manuscripts being circulated at the time of finalizing the official version of the Quran. Caliph Uthman Ibn Affan (576–656 CE) destroyed all unofficial manuscripts to avoid any contention regarding discrepancies in the Quranic text.

6. Abu Bakr was the father of his last wife, Aisha. Ali was the husband of his daughter Fatimah.

7. John 1:1,14

8. Muslims consider the Quran untainted by human influence. However source criticism points to the fact that the Quran borrowed from a number of pre-existing sources such as the Jewish Torah, Christian New Testament, and other Zoroastrian and Arab literatures.

9. Jesus is called Isa twenty-five times, Al- Massih eleven times, and Ibn Miriam twenty-three times.

10. Sura 3:49. The childhood stories of Jesus are originally found in apocryphal literatures such as protoevangelium Jacobi (the Infancy Gospel of James) or the Infancy Gospel of Thomas, which church fathers regarded as "too good to be true."

11. Sura 19:29 -33

12. The Arabic word "kalim" does not have the same theological innuendos as the Greek word "logos." Yet, in Islamic thought, it is through His Word that God creates and sustains the universe and reveals His will to the world.

13. Sura 3:45 and 4:171. Some Muslims wrongly say that kalimatuallah is also used to describe John the Baptist. In reality what the Quran says is that John the Baptist is someone "witnessing the truth of a Word from Allah [kalimatin mina Allāhi], (3:39), which is again a reference to Jesus himself.

14. Jesus is called Christ/Messiah eleven times (for eg. Sura 5:72).

15. In the history of Islam, many charismatic leaders have presented themselves as messiahs with a divine mandate to establish the rule of God. In Iranian Twelver Shiaism, the twelfth Imam, Muhammad Al Muntazar, is the Al-Mahdi, who will return with Al-Masih (Jesus) in the days of the apocalypse.

16. According to traditional belief, Jesus will get married and live a normal life in the world. Once again, the marriage of Jesus with the church is a theological metaphor used in the Bible, which Muslims interpret as a literal marriage.

17. Hadith Al-Zukruh 43:57-67

18. Sura 19:22-27

19. Apostle Paul did a comparison of Jesus and Adam more elaborately in his epistles (1 Corinthians 15:45-49). Paul described Jesus as the second or last Adam, in a sense that Jesus transforms our mortal nature inherited from Adam into his divine nature.

20. Sura 3:59

21. Muslim apologists argue that another character in the Bible, Melchizedek, is also described as one without father, mother, or descent, and had neither beginning of days nor end of life (Hebrews 7:3). He appears in a brief passage in Genesis 14 where he is described the king of Salem who met Abraham while returning from a slaughter of the people who captured his nephew Lot. This is again a classic case of theological metaphor. Melchizedek was a type, or a shadow of the eternal High Priest to come. The writer of Hebrews does not say that he actually had no genealogy, but only that it is not recorded in the scriptures.

22. Genesis 2:4-9, Sura 2:30

23. Sura 21:91, Sura 66:12

24. Sura 4:171

25. Sura 2:87

26. Sura 3: 49

27. Sura 19:88-92

28. Sura 6:101

29. More explanation on this term in chapter 7

30. Sura *4:157*

31. The word is similar to doekim (made to appear) from where the heresy of Docetism arises in Gnostic Christianity.

32. The denial of Jesus' crucifixion has its origin in the teachings of apocryphal texts like the Gospel of Barnabas, Acts of John, and others. These documents were widely circulated during the formative years of Islam through the Gnostic Christians, exiled to Arabia by the Byzantine Empire. The Gnostics were charged with their heretical belief in "the unreality of Jesus' suffering." (Cragg, K. (1985). *Jesus and the Muslim: An Exploration.* London, Allen and Unwin. Page 174.) Historians believe that Muhammad "held out an olive branch to Christian Gnostics who denied that Jesus was crucified." (Robinson, N. (1991). *Christ in Islam and Christianity.* Albany, NY, State University of New York Press. Page 110).

33. Sura 3:55

34. Josephus, F. (1987). *The Works of Josephus.* Peabody, MA, Hendrickson. 18:63.

35. Tacitus, C. (2004). *The Annals.* Chicago, Hackett.*15:44*.

36. A small group of Muslim commentators are willing to accept the possibility that Jesus indeed died on the cross as a martyr, though he is always alive to God. Al-Razi notes the tradition which concedes, "I am causing you to die" (*mutawaffika*) to be about the literal death (*mumituka*). There are three different traditions in which this theory was understood: (1) Jesus died for three hours, and then was raised back to life. (2) He died for seven hours and then God restored him to life and raised him. (3) God caused Jesus to die at the moment when he raised him to heaven.

37. Sura *19:33*

38. Sura 2:87

39. There are numerous occasions in which Allah asks Muhammad to confess and repent for his own sins. Sura 40:55/57, 47:19/2, 148:2.

40. Sura 19:19

41. Abu Huraira (Sahih Muslim, Book 030, Number 5837). This hadith has been narrated on the authority of Zuhri with the same chain of transmitters (and the words are):" The newborn child is touched by the Satan (when he comes in the world) and he starts crying because of the touch of Satan."

42. Sura 3:45

43. Genesis 22:1-19

44. Sura 37:101 – 107. It is important to note, however, that the name of the son is not mentioned in the passage.

45. Sura 2:67-71

46. Sura 2:73

47. Sura 37:107

48. Zwemer, S. (1912). *The Moslem Christ*. New York, NY, American Tract Society. Page 78. (Originally a quote from TG Huges).

Chapter 6
THE PIERCED MESSIAH

1. (1) The Abrahamic Covenant: God would give the Jewish people the land of Canaan as their inheritance (Genesis15:18), and through them He would bring ultimate blessing to all nations (Genesis 12:3). (2) The Mosaic Covenant: At Mount Sinai, God gave the Israelites the Law and promised again to give them the Land (Exodus 19). (3) The Davidic Covenant: Psalm 89:3,4 and 2 Samuel 7:12-16 record certain promises God made to King David.

2. A *mitzvot* refers to the 613 commandments given in the Torah and the seven rabbinic commandments instituted later, for a total of 620. The 613 commandments are divided into 365 negative commandments and 248 positive commandments.

3. The gospel writers directly attribute Jesus' sentencing to the Jewish leaders (Matthew 26:3-4, Mark 14:1, Luke 22:2, 4-5, John 11:47-50). Matthew goes further, putting the collective responsibility of Jesus' death on the Jewish nation (Matthew 27:25). Paul describes the Jews as those "who both killed the Lord Jesus and the prophets, and drove us out. They are not pleasing to God, but hostile to all men" (1 Tim 2:15).

4. Excerpt from an article by Nicholas Berdyaev, "Christianity and Anti-Semitism," as noted in Selders, G. (1985). *The Great Thoughts*. New York, Ballantine Books.

5. Nostra Aetete proclaimed by His Holiness Pope Paul VI on October 28, 1965 available at:
http://www.vatican.va/archive/hist_councils/ii_vatican_council/documents/vat-ii_decl_19651028_nostra-aetate_en.html

6. Based on Moltmann, J. (1993). *Theology of Hope*. Minneapolis, Fortress Press.

7. "Debru Emet: A recent statement by Jews on Christianity." (Page 44: Judaism II, TLC).

8. Issued on Dec 3, 2015 it was initially signed by 25 rabbis, but many have added signatures since. The document is available at http://cjcuc.com/site/2015/12/03/orthodox-rabbinic-statement-on-christianity/ accessed on 4/24/2017.

9. Mark 10:45

10. Luke 4:16

11. John 10:22-39

12. Fisher, E. (1993). *Faith Without Prejudice: Rebuilding Christian Attitudes Toward Judaism*, Crossroad.

13. Though Jesus appears to have breached the Jewish rites such as Sabbath, in fact, he was only breaking the legalistic codes of Sabbath written by the scribes, not the commandment of Sabbath itself.

14. Flavius Josephus: *Antiquities of the Jews*, Book 18, Chapter 3, 3 This is one of the most controversial passages in the book as the skeptics think of it as a later insertion by Christians.

15. Itzhaki, Y. (2011). *The Uncovered Head: Jewish Culture*. Newarkk, University of Delaware Press. Page 100.

16. Rabbi Shapiro, R. M. (2004). *Open Secrets: The Letters of Reb Yerachmiel ben Yisrael*. New York, Monkfish.

17. Genesis 18:1

18. Genesis 32:30

19. Joshua 5: 13-15

20. Daniel 3:25

21. God is said to have experienced joy (Isaiah. 65:19), grief (Judges. 10:16), anger (Deuteronomy. 1:37), hatred (Psalms. 5:5-6), and love (Jeremiah. 31:3), among many other examples.

22. Isaiah 7:14

23. 2 Samuel 2: 12 -16

24. Isaiah 45:1

25. Encyclopaedia Judaica, Online Version, https://www.jewishvirtuallibrary.org/jsource/judaica/ejud_0002_0014_0_13744.html accessed on 11/20/2016.

26. Jeremiah 23:6; also 33:16

27. Malachi 4:5-6

28. Zechariah 13, 14

29. "Who is Moshiach?—The Basics." http://www.chabad.org/library/moshiach/article_cdo/aid/1121893/jewish/The-Basics.htm accessed 11/20/2016.

30. Solomon, N. (2014). *Judaism: A Very Short Introduction*. Oxford, Oxford University Press. Page 136

31. http://www.chabad.org/library/moshiach/article_cdo/aid/1121893/jewish/The-Basics.htm accessed 11/20/2016

32. Shai, C. *The Great Courses: Introduction to Judaism*. The Teaching Company. Guidebook, Page 26.

33. Solomon, N. Page 119.

34. Isaiah 7:14, Micah 5:2

35. Isaiah 2:2-3, Isaiah 56:6-7, Ezekiel 37:26,27) (Micah 4:1-4, Hosea 2:20, Isaiah 2:1-4) (Zechariah 3:9, 8:23, 14:9, Isaiah 45:23, Isaiah 66:23, Jeremiah 31:33, Ezekiel 38:23, Psalm 86:9)

36. Zechariah 12:10, cf. John 19:37

37. Isaiah 53:2-6. Many Jewish scholars insist that the suffering servant in Isaiah 53 is a figurative description of Israel. But Rabbi Moshe Alsheich, who lived in Palestine in the sixteenth century, wrote: "Our teachers, blessed be their memory, confirmed and unanimously accepted that this chapter speaks about the King Messiah..., who suffers for the iniquities of the children of Israel, and behold, his reward is with him." Rabbi Eliah De Vidas, who lived in Saphed, Israel, at the end of the sixteenth century: "In the same manner that the Messiah suffers for our iniquities which cause him to be bruised, even ours; if anyone wishes that the Messiah should not be bruised for our transgressions, he himself will suffer and be bruised." Quoted from Santala, R. (1992). "How can we be convinced that Jesus is the Messiah?" Bible talks given in Moscow to Messianic Jews.

38. Patai, R. (1979). *The Messianic Text*. Detroit, Wayne State University Press. Page 166.

39. Jeremiah 31:9, 20

40. Babylonian Talmud Sukkah 52a[8],[9] as quoted by Patai, R. (1979). Page 168.

41. Zechariah 12:10

42. Deuteronomy 16:1-8

43. *Christ in the Passover*. Jews for Jesus. December 2010. https://www.youtube.com/watch?v=gBGz3k37kDE

44. In some versions the egg represents new beginnings.

45. The bread is pierced before rolling it and later baked in high temperature. Each matzo becomes striped and pierced in the process.

46. The ritual itself suggests that the bread represents the unity of the triune God. If it represents the unity of worship (priest, Levites, people) or the unity of the patriarchs (Abraham, Isaac, and Jacob), there is no answer to why the second one is broken, buried and brought up.

47. 1 Corinthians 5:7

48. Matthew 26:28

49. In modern Jewish practice, prayer has taken the place of sacrifice. Jewish people believe that the purposes of sacrifice and prayer are similar: to praise God, to become closer to Him, to express thanksgiving, love or gratitude.

50. Leviticus 16:15-22

51. Mishnah Torah, Laws of Teshuvah 1:3. http://www.chabad.org/library/article_cdo/aid/911888/jewish/Teshuvah-Chapter-One.htm accessed 11/20/2016.

52. Solomon, N. Page 63.

53. Genesis 2:16-17, Ezekiel 18:20, Romans 6:23, Hebrews 10:1-12

54. Revelations 13:8 John 1:29

55. Quoted from Rabbi Mordechai, K. (2000). _Understanding Judaism: A Basic Guide to Jewish Faith, History, and Practice._ New York, Mesorah. Page 102

Chapter 7
THE EMPTIED GOD

1. Frank Viola. Interview with Bono. October 3, 2016. http://www.patheos.com/blogs/frankviola/bono-on-jesus/ accessed 11/20/2016.

2. Lewis, C. S. (1952). _Mere Christianity._ New York, Harper Collins.

3. Matthew 16:13

4. Some may argue that this name has prophetic connotations to an eschatological figure we find in the book of Daniel. Daniel 7:13-14 talks about "one like a son of man," who is standing for "the saints of the Most High" (7:18, 21-22) and who will have dominion over all the earth. This might very well be the case, but for an average audience at the time, the son of man only meant an ordinary person.

5. John 8:24, 58

6. Exodus 3:14

7. John 14:9

8. John 10: 30

9. Mark 2:6-7

10. Virgil, _The Aeneid._ As quoted in Burger, M., Ed. (2015). _Sources for the History of Western Civilization._ Toronto, University of Toronto Press. Page 194.

11. Matthew 16:17

12. Revelations 1: 13 - 18

13. Exhortation to the Greeks 1:7:1 (190 CE).

14. The Flesh of Christ 5:6–7 (210 CE).

15. The Fundamental Doctrines 1:0:4 (230 CE)).

16. Although the council of Nicaea was held in 325 CE, the Nicene creed is believed to have been composed much later in 381 CE.

17. Council of Chalcedon 451 CE

18. Attributed to Athanasius of Alexandria (296 – 373 CE)

19. Some would argue that Jesus as a created being based on his title as the "Firstborn of creation" Revelations 1:5 _"the firstborn of the dead"_ Colossians 1:18 _"the firstborn from the dead,"_ Romans 8:29 _"He would be the firstborn among many brethren"_ First born is a title that shows privilege, it does not always have something to do with the birth order. (Esau's firstborn title is sold to Jacob) Hebrews 1:2 _"In these last days has spoken to us in His Son, whom He appointed heir of all things, through whom also He made the world."_ In the case of Jesus, the title 'first born' is mostly a metaphorical usage to describe his power and authority.

20. Lewis, C. S. (1952). _Mere Christianity._ New York, Harper Collins. Page 157

21. Isaiah 6:1-13
22. John 12: 37-43
23. Isaiah 6:10. Also in 44:18
24. Exodus 33:18-23
25. Hebrews 11:26
26. John 10:33
27. John 16:30, John 21:17
28. John 6:64
29. Matthew 18:20
30. Matthew 8: 26-27
31. 1 Timothy 1:17, Colossians 1:15, 2 Corinthians 4:4, Hebrews 1:3, Colossians 2:9
32. Titus 2:13. 1 John 5:20, 2 Peter 1:1, Revelations 1:8, 22:12
33. Bill Maher in Charles, L. (2009). *Riligulous*, Lions Gate.
34. 2 Corinthians 5:19
35. 1 John 4:8
36. The true opposite of love is 'apathy,' not 'wrath.' Wrath is nothing but another expression of God's love.
37. Viola interview with Bono.
38. Matthew 16:25, 2 Corinthians 12:10
39. Dunstan, S. (1991). You, Lord, Are Both Lamb and Shepherd. *United Church Hymn Book*, GIA.

Chapter 8
THE ONLY WAY

1. Lewis, C. S. (1945). "Christian Apologetics," in *God in the Dock*.
2. Lewis, C. S. (1945). "Myth Becomes Fact" in *God in the Dock*.
3. Lewis, C. S. (1945). "Christian Apologetics," in *God in the Dock*.
4. "These "primordial images" or "archetypes," as I have called them, belong to the basic stock of the unconscious psyche and cannot be explained as personal acquisitions. Together they make up that psychic stratum which has been called the collective unconscious." Jung, Carl. (1960) *Collected Works vol. 8*, (1929) The Significance of Constitution and Heredity in Psychology. 229–230 (p. 112).
5. Richardson, D. (1981). *Eternity in Their Hearts*. Ventura, Regal. Page 56.
6. Ibid.
7. Psalms 19:1
8. Acts 14: 16, 17–16
9. Romans 2:15
10. Romans 2:14
11. Based on NOSTRA AETATE at Vatican 2.

12. Olson, R. (2006). "A Wind that Swirls Everywhere." *Christianity Today.* 50. Page 52.
13. 2 Timothy 3:16
14. Colossians 1:15
15. For example, Judaism, which abhors any representations of God in a physical form, can never be "one" with Hinduism, which portrays God in every possible shape and form.
16. Prothero, S. (2011). *God is Not One: The Eight Rival Religions that Run the World.* New York, Harper One. Page viii.
17. Exodus 20:3
18. Sura 9:30
19. Sura 5:51 and Sura 5:72
20. John 14:6
21. Acts 4:12
22. According to the Center for the Study of Global Christianity (CSGC) at Gordon-Conwell Theological Seminary, 2011.
23. John 6:38
24. Titus 2:11
25. Luke 2:10
26. Karl Barth, Church Dogmatics I/1 and IV.3.
27. Time (1962). Religion: Witness to an Ancient Truth. Time. Friday, Apr. 20
28. Egan, H. D. (1986). *Karl Rahner in Dialogue: Conversations and Interviews.* Michigan, Crossroads.
29. Lewis, C. S. (1952). *Mere Christianity.* New York, Harper Collins.
30. Rig Veda X:121 http://www.sacred-texts.com/hin/sbe32/sbe3215.htm .
31. Revelations 3:20
32. Isaiah 25:6-8

EPILOGUE

1. Brahadaranyaka Upanishads (I. iii. 28).
2. John 1:9

For

Further Exploration

Sign up for an Online Course in

WORLD RELIGIONS

www.themosaiccourse.org

Made in the USA
Columbia, SC
20 April 2019